My Door Is Always Open

D0193333

My Door Is Always Open

A CONVERSATION ON FAITH, HOPE AND THE CHURCH IN A TIME OF CHANGE

POPE FRANCIS
WITH ANTONIO SPADARO

Translated from the Italian by Shaun Whiteside

BLOOMSBURY
LONDON • NEW DELHI • NEW YORK • SYDNEY
In association with *La Civiltà Cattolica*

First published in Great Britain 2014

Copyright © 2013 RCS Libri S.p.A. Milan

Chapter VI original text in Italian (*La Civiltà Cattolica* 2014 I 3–17),
translated into English by Fr. Donald Maldari S. J. and Andrew Rutt
(revised, Jan 6) @La Civiltà Cattolica

The moral right of the author has been asserted

No part of this book may be used or reproduced in any manner
whatsoever without written permission from the Publisher except in the
case of brief quotations embodied in critical articles or reviews. Every
reasonable effort has been made to trace copyright holders of material
reproduced in this book, but if any have been inadvertently overlooked the
Publishers would be glad to hear from them.

A Continuum book

Bloomsbury Publishing Plc
50 Bedford Square
London WC1B 3DP

www.bloomsbury.com

Bloomsbury is a trademark of Bloomsbury Publishing Plc

Bloomsbury Publishing, London, New Delhi, New York and Sydney
A CIP record for this book is available from the British Library.

ISBN 9781472909763

10 9 8 7 6 5 4 3 2 1

Typeset by Fakenham Prepress Solutions, Fakenham, Norfolk NR21 8NN

Printed and bound in Great Britain by CPI Group (UK) Ltd, Croydon
CR0 4YY

MIX
Paper from
responsible sources
FSC
www.fsc.org   FSC® C020471

CONTENTS

Contents

This Book

After 19 September 2013, when the interview with Pope Francis was published in *La Civiltà Cattolica* and fifteen other Jesuit journals in other countries, my life changed in a way. Apart from the media avalanche that I had to deal with, there's only one fact that I'd like to stress: I received over a thousand emails, letters, tweets, texts, phone calls and posts on my Facebook profile from normal people, ordinary people, from all parts of the world, as well as from friends telling me – some in 140 characters, some in long letters – about their experience of the interview.

I have to admit naively that I hadn't expected it, and what I experienced went far beyond anything I could have imagined. Some told me how moved they were; some had left the Church years before, some had even left the priesthood, still others were agnostics who expressed a desire to read the Gospel after reading the interview, some were worried about the Pope's 'openness', still others thanked me for the energy that the Pope's words had given them. But above all I had lots of messages from people who were ill and sensed some hope. When a journalist called it an extraordinary scoop, I felt the need to reply straight away: 'No! It was and remains a great spiritual experience.'

Once during a television debate I said as a joke: 'The experience was so rich that I could write a book about it.' From that moment lots of people seriously encouraged me to do it, and in a hurry. This book is the fruit of those words of encouragement. It contains the text of the interview, with the correction of a few typos. But in reality I see this as an opportunity to revisit the interview while going into greater detail and illustrating its contents. I'll try to explain myself: interviewing Pope Francis is, let's put it this way, impossible. His original answers are rarely brief sentences in reply to a precise question. The Pope is volcanic, he likes to enter into dialogue, to open doors and windows, do an abrupt turn, but above all enter into a dialectic and remember personal details. He doesn't engage in dialogue without referring to some sort of concrete experience. He can write more abstractly, but not when he's involved in a dialogue. His type of reasoning isn't based on abstract concepts, it's a reflection and an exchange about real life. At least that's my experience of three afternoons of dialogue with him.

Our discussion, in its published form, is therefore the reliable and organic trace, revised by the Pope, of a dialogue which, for me, remains an inexhaustible seam of content and information. For various reasons, especially to avoid accumulating too much layered information, anecdotes, gestures, and expressions were left out of the final text... In fact the published interview contains a number of them: I preferred a narrative style so that I had the chance of putting them in. However, others were left out. And also omitted was the specific reference, which emerged in the dialogue, to speeches, homilies and texts that Jorge Mario Bergoglio wrote either as a Jesuit priest or as Cardinal Archbishop of Buenos Aires.

Now, in this definitive edition, I've tried to recover in the form of a comment everything that had gone missing, so as to clarify retrospectively the content of the interview, not only from the cultural and pastoral point of view, but also from the human and biographical perspective. The Pontiff has authorized the restoration of those passages. I have also included a kind of 'behind the scenes' for the interview itself. I've developed a hermeneutics of the words of Pope Francis in the light of the dense weave of texts from prior to his election, and also of his interventions as Pontiff. I have checked that this method can be useful in gaining a better understanding of what the Pope says, particularly in a number of passages which are controversial, or in which he refers to things or events that the reader may not necessarily know.

In its own way, the interview is a little miracle. It emerged from the idea that the editors of the cultural journals of the European Jesuits had, along with those of Chile and Venezuela, of interviewing the Pope. We then invited our American journal to join in, because I knew that its staff planned to send some written questions to the Pope and were wondering how to go about it. So it was a project that implied not only the interview, but also its swift translation into various languages with a view to publication in sixteen journals at the same time. And so it came to pass at 17.00 hours (Roman time) on 19 September 2013. The miracle was certainly the concerted action by all these journals from all over the world, but also the fact that there were no leaks of information – very easy and always possible, given the complexity of the operation that involved whole editorial teams, translators and technicians.

To tell the truth, we knew that a major daily newspaper had come into possession of the whole text about eight hours before its first official release, but also that it would be kept under embargo until 17.00 hours out of respect for the Pope. This too, perhaps, was a miracle: a daily newspaper giving up such a scoop.

**

Since its foundation in 1850, the journal *La Civiltà Cattolica* has always enjoyed a special connection with the Apostolic See, but this is the first time it has published an interview with the Pontiff. We Jesuits on the editorial team – because the editorial team has always been composed entirely of Jesuits – are happy with this event. For my part, I present this book to the reader as if sharing an experience, and with the gratitude of one who is still, thanks to messages from so many people, enjoying a time of grace.

Father Antonio Spadaro S.J.

Santa Marta, Monday 19 August, 9.50 a.m.

It's Monday 19 August 2013. Pope Francis has given me an appointment at 10.00 a.m. in Santa Marta. But I have inherited from my father the need always to turn up early. The people who welcome me offer me a seat in a little drawing room. I don't have to wait for long, and after a few minutes I'm accompanied to the lift. In those two minutes I have had time to remember how, in Lisbon, at a meeting of the editors of some Jesuit journals, the idea had come up of publishing an interview with the Pope all at the same time. I had talked with the other editors, suggesting a few questions that expressed everyone's interests. I leave the lift and see the Pope already waiting for me in the doorway. Or rather, in fact, I had the peaceful sense of not having passed through any doors.

I step into his room, and the Pope offers me a seat in an armchair. He sits on a higher, stiff-backed chair, and talks about the problems he has with his back. The setting is simple, austere. The working space on the desk is small. I'm struck by the basic nature not only of the furniture, but of the things as well. There are few books, few papers, few objects.

Among them an icon of St Francis, a statue of Our Lady of Luján, patron saint of Argentina, a crucifix and a statue of St Joseph asleep, very like the one I saw in his room as rector and Provincial Superior at the Colegio Máximo in San Miguel. Bergoglio's spirituality consists not of 'harmonized energies', as he would call them, but of human faces: Christ, St Francis, St Joseph, Mary.

The Pope welcomes me with the smile that he has shown by now all over the world, the one that opens hearts. We start talking about lots of things, but above all about his trip to Brazil. The Pope sees it as a real grace. I ask him if he has rested. He tells me he has, that he's well, but above all that World Youth Day was a 'mystery' to him. He tells me he's never been used to talking to so many people: 'I can look at individual persons, one at a time, to come into contact in a personal way with the person I have before me. I am not used to the masses.' I tell him it's true, and that it's plain to see, that everyone's struck by it.

You can see that when he's surrounded by people his eyes always rest on individuals. Then the television cameras show the images and everyone can see them, but that way he can feel free to remain in direct contact, at least ocular contact, with whoever he has in front of him. He seems content with that, with being what he is, not having to alter his ordinary way of communicating with others, even when he has six million people in front of him, as happened on the beach at Copacabana.

Before I switch on the tape recorder we talk about other things as well. Commenting on a publication of mine, he told me that the two contemporary French thinkers he prefers are Henri de Lubac and Michel de Certeau. I tell him a few personal things about myself. He talks to me about himself as well, in particular his election to the Pontificate. He tells me that when he began to realize that there was a danger that he might be elected, at lunchtime on Wednesday 13 March, he felt a deep and inexplicable peace and inner consolation descending upon him, along with total darkness, a deep obscurity about everything else. And he took those feelings with him to the election.

I would really have liked to go on talking to him in such intimate terms for some time, but I pick up the sheets of paper with some questions that I've jotted down and turn on the tape recorder. First of all I thank him in the name of all the editors of the Jesuit journals that will publish this interview.

Shortly before the audience that he granted to the Jesuits of *La Civiltà Cattolica* on 14 June 2013, the Pope had talked to me about how difficult he found it to give interviews. He had told me that he prefers thinking rather than throwing out off-the-cuff answers in interviews. He feels that the right answers come to him after he's given his first reply: 'I didn't recognize myself when on the flight back from Rio de Janeiro I gave answers to the journalists asking me questions,' he tells me. But it's true: several times in the course of this interview the Pope felt free to interrupt what he was saying when he answered a question, to add something about the previous one.

In fact, talking to Pope Francis is a kind of volcanic flow of ideas that connect up together. Even taking notes gives me the disagreeable sense of interrupting a wellspring dialogue. It's clear that Pope Francis is more accustomed to conversations than to giving lessons.

Interviewing Pope Francis

Talking one to one with Pope Francis is a spiritual experience. Being with him for a long period of time gave me the impression of seeing a man deeply immersed in God. One of his friends, Luis Palau, the well-known Evangelical Christian leader, once said of him: 'When you're with Bergoglio you have the feeling that he knows the Lord God personally.' That's how it is. Most of all you feel you're with a free man, a man with a freedom that is spiritual while also being fully involved in life, in its dynamics, in emotions. He is a resolute man who is comfortable in his own skin.

Jorge Mario Bergoglio has a great sense of humour,

but also a sense of the seriousness of life that makes him austere but never gloomy. He is very attentive to those around him, he knows how to immerse himself in their stories. His humanity, a real 'calm chaos', calls for a relationship that is never codified as it must be in a formal interview. So (I can't remember how or why), I talked to him about my parents, Grazia and Santi. He thanked me a lot for that. He talked to me about his grandmother Rosa, of the walks he took with his family, about cinema... All with the tape recorder off, obviously. I had trouble turning it on, as if clicking on that digital switch would circumscribe the meaning of a conversation that had been private until then.

In front of me I had paper and pen. I also started taking notes. That didn't last long either. That white sheet of paper filling up with my scribbles was becoming a barrier, a filter for a conversation that was fluid and pithy. I soon decided to set my pen aside and talk freely with him: the tape recorder would do its work. And the conversation was fluid. Certainly, the Jesuit training also gave us another language in common.

The Pope told me clearly not to worry about raising objections if I heard something that wasn't clear to me, or not shareable. I certainly wasn't about to raise objections to the Pope, but his invitation revealed the desire for a sincere and honest dialogue.

He convinced me of this one detail: the fact that he liked Henri de Lubac and Michel de Certeau. I knew about de Lubac, whom he had quoted several times. I didn't know about de Certeau. These two men were Jesuits who worked closely together.

In 1950 de Certeau became a Jesuit not least because he was inspired by de Lubac, with whom he was in great accord. In 1971, however, de Lubac dissociated himself completely and harshly from his pupil. The fact that Pope Francis now quotes them together, as a pair, strikes me as the sign of a way of thinking that is open to conflict, to divergent and not necessarily reconcilable positions. On 19 September 2009, concluding the XII Jornada de Pastoral at the Colegio San Cayetano de Liniers he had said: 'The biggest danger, the worst illness, is homogeneity of thought, autism of the intellect, of emotion, which leads me to conceive things inside my bubble. So it's important to recover otherness and dialogue.'

But he is also keen on a union of differences, the fact that they can coexist, and for that reason he has come up with an image: the polyhedron 'which is the union of all partialities, which in unity maintains the originality of single partialities'.[1] So I feel very much at ease. But I am distinctly aware of a kind of paradox: I 'know' I'm with the Pope, I am aware of his authority, but I don't feel distanced from him in any way. His authority is not accompanied by hieratic distance, but by close availability, the 'cercanía' so near to his heart.

**

But at one point I had the sense of sitting on a volcano. I told the Pope, and I think he pretended not to hear me. The Pope is a dreamer. Not in the usual sense of someone who believes in dreams. He believes in desires, he certainly believes in those. But he is too practical and concrete a man to be fooled by vague dreams, by nostalgic memories or by what he has called 'nebulous Proustianism'.

It is rather that he believes in dreams in terms of places to encounter God, in the Biblical sense. That is where all his energy comes from. Not by chance does the Pope have a statue of a sleeping St Joseph in front of his desk. He even has another, similar one on a table by his bedroom door. This statuette shows the dream in which the angel tells him, 'Do not be afraid to take Mary, your wife' (Mt. 1.20).[2] This strikes me as the best image of his action and his ministry: Joseph's dream and the 'unshakeable obedience'[3] that followed from it.

'Do not be afraid to...': it must be that inner certainty that accompanied his acceptance, full of consolation, but also a sense of obscurity about what

13

would happen in the future, as he told me. From that moment everything became a surprise for him, as it was for St Joseph. 'It is the Lord who fills the public squares', he told me at one point in the interview, 'in Rio or in Rome. And everything is a surprise for me. I even surprise myself', he says to me. A 'sympathy' was established with people, and in reality it is something much more profound.

It is the sympathy of which Abraham Joshua Heschel speaks, and which concerns the prophet, who harmonizes his life with the Word of God, involving the feelings of those who listen to him.[4] And St Joseph is also the link with an experience of life marked by 'guardianship'.

On 19 March, the saint's feast day, during the mass inaugurating his Petrine ministry, Francis had said he felt as if it was his specific task to be a 'guardian' like Joseph himself, to live 'in constant attention to God, open to signs', capable of 'reading events realistically', of being 'aware of what is going on around him', of 'taking the wisest decisions'.

And for Bergoglio that awareness means always knowing that 'God surprises us'. His question is: 'Should I allow God to surprise me, as Mary did, or close myself up in my certainties, material certainties, intellectual certainties, ideological certainties, certainties of my plans?'[5]

With the microphone still turned off, I tell Pope Francis that many of his gestures remind me of Pope Marcellus II (1501–55), a pontiff greatly loved by St Ignatius. His pontificate, very short – less than a month – because of his premature death, had suddenly awoken many hopes of Church reform. Today he is also remembered because Palestrina, one of the greatest composers of the day, composed for him one of the greatest pieces of polyphonic music, the so-called 'Missa Papae Marcelli'.

I have with me some official letters that the Society wrote about this pope. I read him some fragments that relate how, shortly after his election he 'forbade the usual signs of joy in Castel Sant'Angelo and other places, and he ordered that the money usually spent on such feasts be given to the poor and to pious works'. And hence also that Pope Marcello loved 'always to go to the Church of St Peter's and the palace chapel on foot rather than in the gestatorial chair'.

I try to work out whether it's true, whether he recognizes himself in this parallelism. 'His pontificate lasted barely a month' is the only comment from the Pope, who smiles as he says it, 'and he was followed by Cardinal Carafa'. And it should be noted that Cardinal Gian Pietro Carafa, elected with the name of Paul IV, is often remembered as the one who extended the powers of the Inquisition and in 1559 he published the first Index of Prohibited Books.

15

Who is Jorge Mario Bergoglio?

I have a question ready, but decide not to follow the outline I had set myself, and ask him more or less off the cuff: 'Who is Jorge Mario Bergoglio?' The Pope stares at me in silence. I ask him if it's a legitimate question to ask him… He gives a sign of accepting the question and says to me: 'I do not know what might be the most fitting description… I am a sinner. This is the most accurate definition. It is not a figure of speech, a literary genre. I am a sinner.'

The Pope goes on thinking, fully aware, as if he hadn't expected that question, as if another thought had come to him. 'Yes, perhaps I can say that I am a bit astute, that I can adapt to circumstances, but it is also true that I am a bit naïve. Yes, but the best summary, the one that comes more from the inside and I feel most true is this: I am a sinner whom the Lord has looked upon.' And he repeats: 'I am a sinner who is looked upon by the Lord. I always felt my motto, *Miserando atque Eligendo* [By Having Mercy and by Choosing Him], was very true for me.'

Pope Francis's motto is taken from the Homilies of the Venerable Bede, who writes in his comments on the Gospel story of the calling of St Matthew:

'Jesus saw a publican, and since he looked at him with feelings of love and chose him, he said to him, "Follow me".' The Pope adds: 'I think the Latin gerund *miserando* is impossible to translate in both Italian and Spanish. I like to translate it with another gerund that does not exist: *misericordiando* ["mercy-ing"].'

Pope Francis continues his reflection and says, jumping to another topic whose meaning I don't immediately understand: 'I do not know Rome well. I know a few things. These include the Basilica of St Mary Major; I always used to go there.' I laugh and say to him: 'We all understood that very well, Holy Father!' 'That's right', the Pope goes on, 'I know St Mary Major, St Peter's... but when I had to come to Rome, I always stayed in [the neighbourhood of] Via della Scrofa. From there I often visited the Church of St Louis of France, and I went there to contemplate the painting of "The Calling of St Matthew" by Caravaggio.' I start to guess what the Pope is trying to tell me.

'That finger of Jesus, pointing at Matthew. That's me. I feel like him. Like Matthew.' And here the Pope becomes determined, as if he had finally found the image he was looking for: 'It is the gesture of Matthew that strikes me: he holds on to his money as if to say, "No, not me! No, this money is mine". Here, this is me, a sinner on whom the Lord has turned his gaze. And this is what I said when they asked me if I would accept my election as Pontiff.' Then the Pope whispers in Latin: 'I am a sinner, but I trust in the infinite mercy and patience of our Lord Jesus Christ, and I accept in a spirit of penance.'

Why did he become a Jesuit?

I understand that the acceptance form was also an identity card for Pope Francis. There was nothing else to add. I go on with what I had chosen as my first question: 'Holy Father, what made you choose to join the Society of Jesus? What struck you about the Jesuit order?'

'I wanted something more. But I did not know what. I entered the diocesan seminary. I liked the Dominicans and I had Dominican friends, but then I chose the Society of Jesus, which I knew well because the seminary was entrusted to the Jesuits. Three things in particular struck me about the Society: the missionary spirit, community, and discipline. And this is strange, because I am a really, really undisciplined person. But the Jesuits' discipline, the way they manage their time – these things struck me very much.

'And then something that is really essential for me is community. I had always sought community, and did not see myself as a priest on my own. I need community. And you can see this by the fact that I am here in Santa Marta. Prior to being elected I was staying in Room 207 [the rooms were assigned by drawing lots]. This room where we are now was a guest room. I chose to live here, in Room 201, because when I took possession of the papal apartments, within me, I heard a distinct "no". The papal apartment in the Apostolic Palace is not luxurious. It is old, tastefully decorated and large, but not luxurious. In addition, it is like an inverted funnel; it might be big and spacious, but the entrance is really narrow. People can only come in dribs and drabs, and I cannot live without people. I need to live my life with others.'

As the Pope talks about mission and community, I think of all those documents of the Society of Jesus that speak of 'community for mission', and I hear them in his words.

What does it mean for a Jesuit to be Pope?

I want to pursue that line and ask the Pope a question based on the fact that he is the first Jesuit to be elected Bishop of Rome: 'How do you understand the role of service to the universal Church that you have been called to play in the light of Ignatian spirituality? What does it mean for a Jesuit to be elected Pope? What element of Ignatian spirituality helps you live your ministry?'

'Discernment', he replies. 'Discernment is one of the things that worked inside St Ignatius. For him it is an instrument of struggle in order to know the Lord and follow him more closely. I was always struck by a saying that describes the vision of Ignatius: *non coerceri a maximo, sed contineri a minimo divinum est* ("not to be limited by the greatest and yet to be contained in the tiniest – this is the divine"). I thought a lot about this phrase in connection with the issue of different roles in the government of the Church, about becoming the superior of somebody else: it is important not to be restricted by a larger space, and it is important to be able to stay in restricted spaces. This virtue of the large and small is magnanimity. Thanks to magnanimity, we can always look at the horizon from the position where we are. That means being able to do the little things of every day with a big heart open to God and to others. That means being able to appreciate the small things inside large horizons, those of the Kingdom of God.

'This motto', the Pope continues, 'offers parameters to assume a correct position for discernment, in order to hear the things of God from God's "point of view". According to St Ignatius, great principles must be embodied in the circumstances of place, time and people. In his own way, John XXIII adopted this attitude with regard to the government of the Church, when he repeated the motto, "See everything; turn a blind eye to much; correct a little". John

21

XXIII saw all things, the maximum dimension, but he chose to correct a few, the minimum dimension. You can have large projects and implement them by means of a few of the smallest things. Or you can use weak means that are more effective than strong ones, as Paul also said in his First Letter to the Corinthians.

'This discernment takes time. For example, many think that changes and reforms can take place in a short time. I believe that we always need time to lay the foundations for real, effective change. And this is the time of discernment. Sometimes discernment instead urges us to do precisely what you had at first thought you would do later. And that is what has happened to me in recent months. Discernment is always done in the presence of the Lord, looking at the signs, listening to the things that happen, the feeling of the people, especially the poor. My choices, including those related to the day-to-day aspects of life, like the use of a modest car, are related to a spiritual discernment that responds to a need that arises from looking at things, at people, and from reading the signs of the times. Discernment in the Lord guides me in my way of governing.

'But I am always wary of decisions made hastily. I am always wary of the first decision, that is, the first thing that comes to my mind if I have to make a decision. This is usually the wrong thing. I have to wait and assess, looking deep into myself, taking the necessary time. The wisdom of discernment redeems the necessary ambiguity of life and helps us find the most appropriate means, which do not always coincide with what looks great and strong.'

The Society of Jesus

'The Society of Jesus is an institution in tension,' the Pope replied, 'always fundamentally in tension. A Jesuit is a person who is not centred in himself. The Society itself also looks to a centre outside itself; its centre is Christ and his Church. So if the Society centres itself in Christ and the Church, it has two fundamental points of reference for its balance and for being able to live on the margins, on the frontier. If it looks too much in upon itself, it puts itself at the centre as a very solid, very well "armed" structure, but then it runs the risk of feeling safe and self-sufficient.

'The Society must always have before itself the *Deus semper maior*, the always-greater God, and the pursuit of the ever greater glory of God, the Church as true bride of Christ our Lord, Christ the king who conquers us and to whom we offer our whole person and all our hard work, even if we are clay pots, inadequate. This tension takes us out of ourselves continuously. The tool that makes the Society of Jesus not centred in itself, really strong, is, then, the account of conscience, which is at the same time paternal and fraternal, because it helps the Society to fulfil its mission better.'

Here the Pope is referring to a specific point in the Constitutions of the Society of Jesus that the Jesuit must 'manifest his conscience', that is, his inner spiritual situation, so that the superior can be more aware and better-informed about sending a person on his mission.

'But it is difficult to speak of the Society', continues Pope Francis. 'When you express too much, you run the risk of being misunderstood. The Society of Jesus can be described only in narrative form. Only in narrative form do you discern, not in a philosophical or theological explanation, which allows you rather to discuss. The style of the Society is not shaped by discussion, but by discernment, which of course presupposes discussion as part of the process. The mystical dimension of discernment never defines its edges and does not complete the thought. The Jesuit must be a person whose thought is incomplete, in the sense of open-ended thinking. There have been periods in the Society in which Jesuits have lived in an environment of closed and rigid thought, more instructive-ascetic than mystical: this distortion of Jesuit life gave birth to the *Epitome Instituti*.'

Here the Pope is referring to a compendium, made for practical purposes, which came to be seen as a replacement for the *Constitutions*. The formation of Jesuits was for some time shaped by this text, to the extent that some never read the *Constitutions*, the foundational text. During this period, in the Pope's view, the rules threatened to overwhelm the spirit, and the Society yielded to the temptation to explicate and define its charism too narrowly.

Pope Francis continues. 'No, the Jesuit always thinks, again and again, looking at the horizon toward which he must go, with Christ at the centre. This is his real strength. And that pushes the Society to be searching, creative and generous. So now, more than ever, the Society of Jesus must be contemplative in action, must live a profound closeness to the whole Church as both the "people of God" and "holy mother the hierarchical Church". This requires much humility, sacrifice and courage, especially when you are misunderstood or you are the subject of misunderstandings and slanders, but that is the most fruitful attitude. Let us think of the tensions of the past history, in the previous centuries, about the Chinese rites controversy, the Malabar rites and the Reductions in Paraguay.

'I am a witness myself to the misunderstandings and problems that the Society has recently experienced. Among those there were tough times, especially when it came to the issue of extending to all Jesuits the fourth vow of obedience to the Pope.

What gave me confidence at the time of Fr Arrupe [superior general of the Jesuits from 1965 to 1983] was the fact that he was a man of prayer, a man who spent much time in prayer. I remember him when he prayed sitting on the ground in the Japanese style. For this he had the right attitude and made the right decisions.'

The model: Peter Faber, 'Reformed Priest'

I am wondering if there are figures among the Jesuits, from the origins of the Society to the present date, that have affected him in a particular way, so I ask the Pope who they are and why. He begins by mentioning Ignatius Loyola [founder of the Jesuits] and Francis Xavier, but then focuses on a figure who is not as well known to the general public: Peter Faber (1506–46), from Savoy. He was one of the first companions of St Ignatius, in fact the first, with whom he shared a room when the two were students at the University of Paris. The third roommate was Francis Xavier. Pius IX declared Faber blessed on 5 September 1872, and the cause for his canonization is still open.

The Pope cites an edition of Faber's works, which he asked two Jesuit scholars, Miguel A. Fiorito and Jaime H. Amadeo, to edit and publish when he was Provincial Superior of the Jesuits in Argentina. An edition that he particularly likes is the one by Michel de Certeau. I ask the Pope why he is so impressed by Faber.

'[His] dialogue with all,' the Pope says, 'even the most remote and even with his opponents; his simple piety, a certain naïveté perhaps, his being available straight away, his careful interior discernment, the fact that he was a man capable of great and strong decisions but also capable of being so gentle and loving.'

As Pope Francis lists the personal characteristics of his favourite Jesuit, I realize that Faber really has been a role model for him. Michel de Certeau simply calls Faber the 'reformed priest', for whom interior experience, dogmatic expression and structural reform are inseparable.

So I think I understand that Pope Francis draws inspiration precisely from this kind of reform. Then the Pope continues with a reflection on the true face of the founder of the Society.

'Ignatius is a mystic, not an ascetic', he says. 'It irritates me when I hear that the Spiritual Exercises are "Ignatian" only because they are done in silence. In fact, the Exercises can be perfectly Ignatian also in daily life and without the silence. An interpretation of the Spiritual Exercises that emphasizes asceticism, silence and penance is a distorted one that became widespread even in the Society, especially in the Society of Jesus in Spain. I am rather close to the mystical movement, that of Louis Lallement and Jean-Joseph Surin. And Faber was a mystic.'

The experience of government

What kind of experience in Church government, as a Jesuit superior and then as superior of a province of the Society of Jesus, helped to fully form Fr Bergoglio? The style of governance of the Society of Jesus involves decisions made by the superior, but also extensive consultation with his official advisors. So I ask: 'Do you think that your past government experience can serve you in governing the universal Church?'

After a brief pause for reflection, he responds: 'In my experience as superior in the Society, to be honest, I have not always behaved in that way – that is, I did not always do the necessary consultation. And this was not a good thing. My style of government as a Jesuit at the beginning had many faults. That was a difficult time for the Society: an entire generation of Jesuits had disappeared. Because of this I found myself Provincial when I was still very young. I was only 36 years old. That was crazy. I had to deal with difficult situations, and I made my decisions abruptly and by myself. Yes, but I must add one thing: when I entrust something to someone, I totally trust that person. He or she must make a really big mistake before I rebuke that person. But despite this, eventually people get tired of authoritarianism.

'My authoritarian and quick manner of making decisions led me to have serious problems and to be accused of being ultra-conservative. I lived a time of great interior crisis when I was in Cordova. To be sure, I have never been like Blessed Imelda [a goody-goody], but I have never been a right-winger. It was my authoritarian way of making decisions that created problems.

'I say these things from life experience and because I want to make clear what the dangers are. Over time I learned many things. The Lord has allowed this growth in knowledge of government through my faults and my sins. So as Archbishop of Buenos Aires, I had a meeting with the six auxiliary bishops every two weeks, and several times a year with the council of priests. They asked questions and we opened the floor for discussion. This greatly helped me to make the best decisions. But now I hear some people tell me: "Do not consult too much, and decide by yourself." Instead, I believe that consultation is very important.'

'The consistories [of cardinals], the synods [of bishops] are, for example, important places to make real and active this consultation. We must, however, give them a less rigid form. I do not want token consultations, but real consultations. The consultation group of eight cardinals, this "outsider" advisory group, is not only my decision, but it is the result of the will of the cardinals, as it was expressed in the general congregations before the conclave. And I want to see that this is a real, not ceremonial consultation.'

Companion of Jesus

'I am a sinner.' This is the first definition that Pope Francis gives of himself, complementing it immediately with a reference to redeeming Grace: 'I am a sinner upon whom the Lord has looked.' I didn't plan to ask him the question about his way of defining himself, but it happened on the spur of the moment when I found myself with him. And the Pope didn't evade the issue, but seemed to look inside himself for the most authentic reply. With his answer, he expressed candidly and honestly what he feels to be his deepest identity.

But at the same time he said something else: he defined himself in the light of his spirituality and his choice of life as a Jesuit. In fact, in 1974 Father Jorge Bergoglio had taken part in the XXXII General Congress of the Society of Jesus. The first decree issued by this global assembly of representatives of the Order began with the question: 'What does it mean to be a Jesuit?' The answer was: 'It means recognizing oneself as a sinner, but one called by God to be a companion of Jesus Christ, as Ignatius was.'

So here Pope Francis is speaking of himself in the light of a charisma that deeply touches his identity. But above all, during our discussion, the Pope insisted that this is not a 'literary definition', or a manner of speaking. For him, in fact, the awareness of being a sinner looked upon by the Lord is conveyed by a precise image, that of Matthew, Levi the publican, the tax collector, the sinner, to whom Jesus said simply, 'Follow me'. 'And he rose and followed him' (Mk 2.14).

Jorge Mario Bergoglio has a particular bond with St Matthew. As he himself said, in Rome, given that he lived near the Church of San Luigi dei Francesi, he often went to look at one of the masterpieces of Caravaggio, 'The Calling of St Matthew', in which the blade of light that pierces the dark room seems to represent divine Grace itself. His episcopal motto, *Miserando atque eligendo*, as already mentioned, derives directly from a homily by the English monk the Venerable Bede (673–735) which refers to the same episode: 'Vidit ergo Jesus publicanum et quia miserando atque eligendo vidit, ait illi: Sequere me.'

This homily – a homage to divine mercy – is repro-duced in the Liturgy of the Hours of the feast of St Matthew. And it holds a particular significance in the life and spiritual itinerary of the Pope. In fact, on the feast of St Matthew, on 21 September 1953, the young Jorge Mario, not yet seventeen, experienced the presence of the Lord's love in his life in a very special way. Following a confession, he felt his heart being touched, and became aware of the descent of God's mercy, calling him to the priesthood.

That 21 September he is preparing to celebrate International Students' Day with an outing to the countryside at the start of the southern spring. But first, without really knowing why, he goes to his parish church, the Church of San José de Flores, where he sees a priest he has never seen before, Father Duarte, by whom he is very struck. He takes a seat in the last confessional on the left, facing the altar, and feels driven to confess. At that moment 'something' happens. Jorge Mario becomes aware of his calling to the priesthood. 'A strange thing happened to me during that confession, I don't know what exactly, but it changed my life; I would say I was caught with my guard down.'

He goes on, remembering those moments: 'It was the surprise, the astonishment of an encounter, I realized that they were waiting for me. That's the religious experience: the astonishment of meeting someone who's waiting for you. From that moment, God for me has been the one who "anticipates" you. You're looking for him, but He's the one who finds you first. You want to meet him, but He's the one who meets you first'.[1]

The Pope, recalling those moments, associates them with a precise experience of the mercy of God, which will go with him ever afterwards. Four years will pass before he goes to the seminary, but the decision had been taken.

Recalling those moments shortly before he was ordained a priest in 1969, in a moment 'of great spiritual intensity' he writes a personal confession of faith that makes reference to that particular confession.[2]

> *I want to believe in God the Father, who loves me like a son, and in the Lord Jesus, who has infused my life with his spirit to make me smile and thus bring me to the kingdom of eternal life.*
>
> *I believe in my story, which was moved by God's loving gaze on that spring day, 21 September, when he came to greet me and invite me to follow him.*
>
> *I believe in my pain, barren from selfishness, where I take refuge.*
>
> *I believe in my soul's abjection, which seeks to swallow without giving… Without giving.*

I believe the rest are good, and that I must fearlessly love them, without ever betraying them for my own safety.

I believe in religious life.

I believe I want to love a lot.

I believe in everyday death, burning, which I avoid, but it smiles at me, inviting me to accept it.

I believe in God's patience, welcoming, as good as a summer night.

I believe my father is in heaven with the Lord.

I believe Father Duarte is also there, interceding on behalf of my priesthood.

I believe in Mary, my mother, who loves me and will never leave me alone.

And I await each day's surprise where love, strength, betrayal and sin will manifest themselves, and will accompany me until the final encounter with that marvellous face, which I do not know and which I continuously escape, yet which I want to get to know and love.

Amen.

So the Pope first entered the Metropolitan Seminary in the district of Villa Devoto, on Calle José Cubas. But this was only the first step. The second happened three years later, when he entered the novitiate of the Society of Jesus, on 11 March 1958. Pope Francis is the first Jesuit Pope in history.

Why did Jorge Mario Bergoglio become a Jesuit? In our interview he answers, 'I wanted to do something more'. What drives him is the quest for something greater. If we had to choose a word that expresses the spirituality of St Ignatius I don't think there's any doubt: it's the Latin adverb *magis*, 'more', just as it's typical that the Jesuit motto should be *Ad Maiorem Dei Gloriam*, hard to translate into English, but which can be rendered as 'To the greater glory of God'. 'God always goes beyond', Pope Francis said by way of summary during his audience with the catechists on 28 September 2013. The dynamic of 'more' is typical of the Ignatian vision.

**

The Society of Jesus was founded by St Ignatius of Loyola (1491–1556) and his first companions, who were placed at the service of the Pope to be sent anywhere in the world where there were 'major' emergencies. This complete and immediate availability to the Pope is expressed in the so-called 'fourth vote' that professed Jesuits express in the words, 'Insuper, promitto specialem obedentiam summon pontifici circa missions...'. This is a special vow of obedience to the Pontiff, who can send the Society's members wherever he thinks appropriate. This vow is motivated by the fact that the Pope is the one who has the most universal vision and knows the need for the Ecclesia universa, wherever they may arise. A

35

Pope, then, who is trained in the spirituality of the Society of Jesus, embodies this universality, which is that of his religious vocation.

This dynamic of the 'magis' has been present in Bergoglio since his youth. In concrete terms it assumed the form of a passion to be sent wherever the need was greatest. The significant features of his personality, which appear obvious to the world today, are already there *in nuce* in his Jesuit calling: the demand not to be 'a priest on his own', to live in 'company', in a community, the need to give a missionary and coherent form to his 'undisciplined' temperament.

Since 13 March 2013 journalists have often asked the Jesuits what it means for a Jesuit to be Pope. I couldn't help asking him directly. From our interview it seems clear that Pope Francis maintains that the element of St Ignatius's spirituality that best helps him to experience his Petrine ministry is 'discernment'. Discernment is the spiritual process which distinguishes those spiritual impulses which lead us to God from those which lead us away from him. This applies to the life of each of us, and discernment helps us to make decisions and make choices according to the Gospel.

But it also applies to historical processes. It is a crucial aspect of the vision and action of the world according to the Jesuits, as confirmed by the 34th General Congregation of the Society of Jesus, which was held in 1995: 'In exercising their priestly ministry, the Jesuits try to see what God has already done in the lives of individuals, societies and cultures, and to discern how God will continue that work. Stressing that all human life is illuminated by Grace, this vision of life influences the way in which the ministerial priesthood of the Jesuit in various fields' (no. 177).

Evangelical spiritual discernment thus tries to recognize the presence of the Spirit in human and cultural reality, the seed, already planted, of its presence in events, in sensibilities, in desires, in the deep tensions of people's hearts and social, cultural and spiritual contexts. 'God already lives in our cities',[3] writes Bergoglio. It is an inward attitude that drives us to be inwardly open to dialogue, to encounter, to find God wherever he can be found and not only within boundaries that are narrow or at least well defined and fenced off. Above all he does not fear ambiguity in life and faces it with courage. Actions and decisions, then, are deeply rooted and must be accompanied by careful, meditative, prayerful reading, of the signs of the times, which are everywhere: from a great international event to a letter written by an ordinary member of a congregation.

For Bergoglio, the world is always in movement: the ordinary perspective, with its standards for judging what is important and what is not, doesn't work. The life of the spirit has other criteria, and his ordinary way of making decisions is, as he told me explicitly, the one that Ignatius of Loyola calls the 'Second Time', that is, 'when sufficient clarity and knowledge are received from the experience of consolations and desolations, and from experience in the discernment of various spirits' (Spiritual Exercises, 176).

It is this kind of clarity and knowledge that has always guided Jorge Mario Bergoglio in making his choices. Even when they happen in times of tranquillity, when the soul 'uses its natural faculties in freedom and peace' (ES 177), he waits for that clear knowledge guided by internal consolation.

It is significant that, as the Pope declares, spiritual discernment should also guide his everyday choices, at first sight immediate and spontaneous. One example: when he talked to me about his decision to stay living in Santa Marta, he used the word 'election'. I was struck by the fact that the Pope uses this word which is typical of the language of St Ignatius to indicate a choice that is the result of alert and internal discernment concerning the will of God.

The principle that synthesises this vision is 'Non coerceri maximo, contineri tamen a minimo, divinum est', which might be translated as 'Don't be constrained by bigger things, but be contained in that which is smaller; that is the divine'. The expression is part of a long literary epitaph composed by an anonymous Jesuit in honour of Ignatius of Loyola.

Hölderlin liked it so much that he added it as a motto to his Hyperion. And we know how much Bergoglio loves the work of Hölderlin, so much so that he recited the poet in the original German when he received the cardinals in the Sala Clementina two days after his election.

William Blake could help us understand this epitaph in a handful of lines: 'See a world in a grain of sand / and heaven in a wild flower. / Hold infinity in the palm of your hand / and eternity in an hour.'

What does Pope Francis mean? That within the horizon of the Kingdom of God the infinitesimal can be infinitely great, and immensity can be a page. The great project is realized in the tiny gesture, the little step: 'God is hidden in what is small and in what is growing, even if we are not capable of seeing it.'[4]

It isn't new, but it is a thought that has accompanied Bergoglio at least since the years in which he was a provincial superior and, in 1981, wrote an essay entitled 'Conducir en lo grande y en lo pequeño', collected today in 'Meditaciones para religiosos'[5] and which the Pope still thinks about and, I have noticed, quotes implicitly in our dialogue.

**

Discernment, then is a fundamental key to understanding the way in which Pope Francis lives out his ministry rooted in the spirituality for which he has been trained. But on the other hand, I have come to understand, after rereading it several times, that this first section of the interview is perhaps the most important when it comes to understanding Bergoglio, because when he talks about the Jesuits he is obviously talking about himself.

And this is the key definition that Pope Francis gives of the Jesuit (and hence of himself): 'A person whose thought is incomplete, whose thought is open.' And again: 'The Jesuit always thinks again and again, looking to the horizon, toward which he must advance, with Christ at the centre.' This is a passage which is, in my opinion, of capital importance. Let us try and gain a better understanding of it.

Many people believe that the Pope has all the clear, distinct ideas, and they wonder where he wants to take the Church. Many think he has a clear starting point and a clear destination, and they wonder about his strategies and objectives. There is nothing wrong about this way of thinking, and yet it is not the dynamic of Bergoglian thought, and of the action which it is capable of generating.

The Pope has a clear idea of context, of the starting situation. However, the road that he seeks to travel is truly open for him; it is not contained in a road map written *a priori*: the path opens up as one travels it. As he said in a letter to priests on 29 July 2007, we must be careful that the horizon does not come so close as to become a fence. The horizon must be truly open.

So the Pope, in consultation and in prayer, enters into a dynamic of discernment that opens him up to the future – even to the future of Church reform, which is not a project but an exercise of the spirit. And the means used by Bergoglio are never merely functional, as he said to me with particular reference to the action of the Jesuits: 'The instrumentality of the Society', he clarifies, 'must not be functional, but mystical: what matters is not efficiency, but mystery.'

In this sense Pope Francis is a man whose thoughts are 'incomplete, open'. And this requires, as he himself affirms in the course of the interview, on the one hand 'research, creativity, generosity', and on the other 'humility, sacrifice, courage'. This attitude is especially called upon in difficult times.

In his interview the Pontiff refers to a complex question of which he was a direct witness, concerning a period in which Father Pedro Arrupe (1907–91) was General of the Society of Jesus. But he also refers to Chinese and Malabar rites and to the Reductions in Paraguay. The question of rites is linked to the figures of Matteo Ricci (1552–1610) and Roberto de Nobili (1577–1656), true pioneers. In fact, in their missions the Jesuits tried to adapt the announcement of the Gospel to local culture and cults. But that worried some people, and voices were raised in the Church contrary to the spirit of these attitudes, as if they involved a contamination of the Christian message.

Incomprehension concerned above all the tolerance of honours paid to deceased ancestors, which could be seen as having the character of an actual cult, and the way of designating God through titles such as 'Heaven', which could be misunderstood. In such questions of a 'prophetic' nature, the Society assumed positions which were not accepted at the time because they went beyond the ordinary understanding of the facts. So even the adventure of the 'Reductions' in Paraguay, the indigenous communities which were organized by the Jesuits and which became increasingly autonomous until they were attacked and suppressed by a Hispano-Portuguese expedition.

'In these cases the Jesuit must not let himself be

blocked by the formulation of negative judgments, but accept them, experience them through prayer and enter into open dialogue to understand where the problem or the ambiguity lies', the Pope said to me. Sometimes it isn't easy, as in the cases he quoted to me. They are all situations and challenges that have been seen at work by figures such as Pedro Arrupe, Matteo Ricci and Roberto de Nobili, men of incomplete and open thought.

For Bergoglio, the horizon and, at the same time, the centre of this incompleteness is always Christ. For Pope Francis, the Society of Jesus is itself only if it has Christ at its centre, as can be read in the Formula of the Institute, which begins by addressing 'whoever desires to serve as a soldier of God beneath the banner of the cross in our Society which we desire to be designated with the name of Jesus, and to serve the Lord alone and the Church his spouse, under the Roman pontiff, the Vicar of Christ on Earth'.

Pope Francis, specifically addressing the Jesuits during Mass on the feast of St Ignatius, on 31 July 2013, said among other things: 'Our crest as Jesuits is a monogram, the acronym of "Iesus Hominum Salvator" (IHS). Each one of you will be able to say to me: we are well aware of that! But this crest continuously reminds us of a reality that we must never forget: the centrality of Christ for each of us and for the Society as a whole, which St Ignatius himself wanted to call "of Jesus" to indicate its reference point. Besides, at the very beginning of the Spiritual Exercises he places us before our Lord Jesus Christ, our Creator and Saviour. And this leads us Jesuits and the Society as a whole to be "decentred", and to have before us "Christ always greater", "Deus semper maior", the "intimior intimo meo" that always takes us outside ourselves, leads us to a certain kenosis, to "leave our own love, want and interests".

The question for us, for all of us, remains: Is Christ the centre of my life? Am I really putting Christ at the centre of my life? Because there is always the temptation to think of ourselves at the centre. And when a Jesuit places himself, not Christ, at the centre, he is in error.'

In this sense for Bergoglio we must be first of all 'mystical' and not 'ascetic'. In the Society itself it becomes clear how he discerns two threads that we might define, perhaps too perfunctorily, as those of ascetic rigorousness and instructive explication; and that of open mysticism and experiential narrative.

**

A synthesis of the Bergoglian vision, the figure who is almost a role model, appears in the form of Peter Faber (1506–46), the first companion of Ignatius of Loyola. He is the 'reformed priest' who appears to sum up the characteristics of a spiritual man which are dear to Bergoglio: a man of discernment, of great gentleness, open-mindedness and capacity for dialogue, but also ready to take big decisions. Faber is above all convinced that at the level of the complexity of feelings and spiritual affects in which man learns to converse with God and feel his mystery, big decisions are taken.

Far from Bergoglio (and Faber), what he himself has called 'the constant temptation of pseudomystical tendencies of the Christian life'.[6] Far from him, 'that sort of spiritual Christianity that was losing contact with everyday, concrete life'.[7] Bergoglio fears excessive trust 'in the exaltation of the emotional element'.[8]

On the other hand, what he knows, above all through his spiritual training, is, as Ignatius writes in his Spiritual Exercises, that God communicates with each of us through internal 'movements' (SE, 313–36), 'he moves and attracts the will' (SE, 175). This space of encounter and attraction, emotionally rich, does not in fact contradict either reason or the running of life and its practical projects, but on the contrary animates it: 'The heart marries the idea to the reality', Bergoglio writes.[9]

It is fascinating to note, for example, the degree to which inner experience and structural reforms are intimately interconnected for Faber. And so they are for Pope Francis.

Let us remember here that when we speak of 'reform' with reference to Faber, we are referring to his broad, deep dialogue with Protestants, even taking part in the Diets of Worms and Regensburg (1540–41), and finally being called by Pope Paul III to take part in the Council of Trent as a theologian, even though, soon after his arrival in the city, he died as a result of the exhausting labours to which he had been subjected. Faber's experience should be understood and studied if one wishes to understand the style of government of Jorge Mario Bergoglio.

Finally, to complete a rich and complex personal portrait, a reflection on his manner of government emerges directly out of the dialogue with Pope Francis. As the Pope himself reminds us, his first experience of government was within the Society of Jesus, in 1973, as the very young Provincial of Argentina.

At the end of the 1960s the Society of Jesus had been shaken very strongly by the spirit of 1968, in terms of people leaving the order. It might be said that a generation went missing, and Father Bergogilio was made Provincial at an unusual age, which is to say that he was too young. At the start of his mandate, and in truly turbulent contexts,

Bergoglio took decisions in a brusque and person-alistic manner.

Then, however, that style of decision-making made him look like an ultra-conservative. It is hard to recognize in his words the Pope we now see acting and speaking. But, the Pontiff adds today, 'I was never on the right'. There is no point in making inferences and deductions on the basis of these words outside their historical context. Let us not forget that in his interview with Sergio Rubin and Francesca Ambrogetti he had also said, 'I was never a Communist'.[10]

It is not then a question of being on the right or left in an ideological, abstract sense. Pope Francis always speaks with reference to experience: either his own or that of his interlocutors. He doesn't speak in vague abstractions. Because of his attitude he has been accused of being on the far right. And he has never been. Here the reference is obviously linked to the historical context, whether political or ecclesiastic, that he himself has experienced.

And let us remember the accusations of conniving with the Argentine dictatorship, which were later denied and refuted.[11] In short, the Pope's affirmation cannot be generalized, as if he were bound to a precise political direction. In fact, what appears quite clear is that Francis is acting in such a way that the rigid pigeonholes of progressiveness or conservatism appear obsolete: they no longer apply.

But above all, any 'devout' attitude that does not imply a true conversion and an adherence to the Gospel now reveals its vanity. Similarly fatuous is any propensity to resolve the question of faith in the Enlightenment forms of champagne socialism. And Bergoglio's first objection would simply be: they don't pray.

During his time as Provincial of the Jesuits in Argentina, Bergoglio, to his own cost, learned that stable, lasting decisions are not taken by instinct and, as we have seen, through discernment he learned not to trust to impulse. That cost him a great deal. The Pope mentioned to me a time of great and dramatic internal crisis. And paradoxically it was at that moment that he was appointed bishop. In conclusion, he himself admits with consolation and spiritual joy that 'the Lord has allowed this pedagogy of government through my defects and my sins'. His initial words come back: 'I am a sinner who is looked upon by the Lord.'

'Thinking with the Church'

I stick to the subject of the Church and try to understand precisely what the 'think with the Church' of which St Ignatius writes in his Spiritual Exercises means for the Pope. He replies without hesitation, starting with an image.

'The image of the Church I like is that of the holy, faithful people of God. This is the definition I often use, which is the image of *Lumen gentium*, no. 12. Belonging to a people has a strong theological value. In the history of salvation, God has saved a people. There is no full identity without belonging to a people. No one is saved alone, as an isolated individual, but God attracts us looking at the complex web of relationships that take place in the human community. God enters into this popular dynamic.

'The people themselves are the subject. And the Church is the people of God on the journey through history, with joys and sorrows. *Sentire cum Ecclesia* [to think and to feel with the Church], therefore, is my way of being a part of this people. And all the faithful, considered as a whole, are infallible in matters of belief, and the people display this *infallibilitas in credendo*, this infallibility in believing, through a supernatural sense of the faith of all the people walking together. This is what I understand today as the "thinking with the Church" of which St Ignatius speaks. When the dialogue among the people and the bishops and the Pope goes down this road and is genuine, then it is assisted by the Holy Spirit. So this thinking with the Church does not concern theologians only.

'This is how it is with Mary: If you want to know who she is, you ask theologians; if you want to know how to love her, you have to ask the people. In turn, Mary loved Jesus with the heart of the people, as we read in the *Magnificat*. We should not even think, therefore, that "thinking with the Church" means only thinking with the hierarchical part of the Church.'

And the Pope, pausing for a moment, emphasizes the following point to avoid any misunderstanding: 'And, of course, we must be very careful not to think that this *infallibilitas* of all the faithful I am talking about in the light of Vatican II is a form of populism. No, it is the experience of the "holy mother the hierarchical Church", as St Ignatius called it, the Church as the people of God, pastors and people together. The Church is the totality of the people of God.

'I see the sanctity of the people of God; this daily sanctity', the Pope continues. 'There is a "middle class of sanctity" which we can all be part of, the holiness Malègue wrote about.'

The Pope is referring to Joseph Malègue, a favourite French writer of his, who was born in 1876 and died in 1940 – in particular to his unfinished trilogy *Pierres noires. Les Classes moyennes du salut.* Some French critics called him 'the Catholic Proust'.

'I see holiness', the Pope continues, 'in the patience of the people of God: a woman who is raising children, a man who works to bring home the bread, the sick, the elderly priests who have so many wounds but have a smile on their faces because they have served the Lord, the sisters who work hard and live a hidden sanctity. This is for me the sanctity that we have in common. I often associate sanctity with patience: not only patience as *hypomoné*, taking responsibility for the events and circumstances of life, but also as a constancy in going forward, day by day. This is the sanctity of the *Iglesia militante* also mentioned by St Ignatius. This was the sanctity of my parents: my father, my mother, my grandmother Rosa who did so much good for me. In my breviary I have the last will of my grandmother Rosa, and I read it often. For me it is like a prayer. She is a saint who suffered so much, also spiritually, and yet always carried on with courage.

'This Church with which we should be thinking and feeling is the home of all, not a small chapel that can only hold a small group of select people. We must not reduce the bosom of the universal Church to a nest protecting our mediocrity. And the Church is Mother; the Church is fruitful. It must be. You see, when I hear of reprehensible behaviour of ministers of the Church, or in consecrated men or women, the first thing that comes to mind is: "Here's an unfruitful bachelor" or "Here's a spinster". They are neither fathers nor mothers. They have not been able to give spiritual life. In contrast, for example, when I read the life of the Salesian missionaries who went to Patagonia, I read a story of life, of fruitfulness.

'Another recent example which made the newspaper headlines, the phone call I made to a young man who wrote a letter to me. I called him because his letter was so beautiful, so simple. For me this was an act of fruitfulness. I realized that he was a young man who is growing up, that he saw a father figure in me, and that his letter communicates something of his life to that father. The father cannot say, "I do not care". This type of fruitfulness does me so much good.'

Churches young and old

I stay on the subject of the Church, asking the Pope a question in the light of the recent International Youth Day: 'This great event recently cast a spotlight on young people, but also on those "spiritual lungs" that are Churches most recently instituted. What hopes for the universal Church do you think these Churches provide?'

'The young Churches have developed a synthesis of faith, culture and life, and so it is a different synthesis from the one developed by the ancient Churches. For me, the relationship between the ancient Churches and the young ones is similar to the relationship between the young and the elderly in a society. Together, they build the future: the young ones with their strength and the older ones with their wisdom. You always run certain risks, of course. The younger Churches are likely to feel self-sufficient; the more ancient ones are likely to want to impose on the younger Churches their cultural models. But we are building the future together.'

The Church as field hospital...

Pope Benedict XVI, announcing his resignation from the pontificate, portrayed today's world as subject to rapid changes, and concerned with questions of great relevance to the life of the faith that require strength from both body and soul. I ask the Pope, in the light of what he has just said to me: 'What does the Church most need at this historic moment? Are reforms needed? What are your wishes for the Church of the coming years? What Church do you dream of?'

Pope Francis, picking up the introduction to my question, begins by saying: 'Pope Benedict did an act of holiness, greatness, humility. He is a man of God', showing great affection and immense respect for his predecessor.

'I see clearly', the Pope continues, 'what the Church needs most today, and it is the ability to heal wounds and to warm the hearts of the faithful, together with closeness, and proximity. I see the Church as a field hospital after battle. It is useless to ask a seriously injured person if he has high cholesterol and about the level of his blood sugars! You have to heal his wounds. Then we can talk about everything else. Heal the wounds, heal the wounds... And you have to start from the ground up.

'The Church has sometimes locked itself up in excessive attention to detail, in small-minded rules. The most important thing is the first proclamation: Jesus Christ has saved you. And the ministers of the Church must be ministers of mercy above all. The confessor, for example, is always in danger of being either too much a rigorist, or too lax. Neither are merciful, because neither of these roles really takes responsibility for the person. The rigorist washes his hands and leaves it to the commandment. The lenient minister washes his hands by simply saying "This is not a sin", or something similar. In pastoral ministry we must accompany people, and we must heal their wounds.

'How are we treating the people of God? I dream of

a Church that is both Mother and Shepherdess. The Church's ministers must be merciful, take responsibility for the people and accompany them like the good Samaritan, who washes, cleans and raises up his neighbour. This is pure Gospel. God is greater than sin. The structural and organizational reforms are secondary – that is, they will come afterwards. The first reform must be that of approach. The ministers of the Gospel must be those who can warm the hearts of the people, who walk through the dark night with them, who know how to dialogue, and to descend themselves into their people's night, into the darkness, but without losing themselves. The people of God want pastors, not bureaucrats, or clergy acting like government officials. The bishops, particularly, must be men able to support the movement of God among their people with patience, so that no one is left behind. But they must also be able to accompany the flock that has a flair for finding new paths.'

'Instead of being just a Church that welcomes and receives by keeping the doors open, let us also try to be a Church that finds new roads, that is able to step outside itself and go to those who do not attend Mass, to those who have quit or are indifferent. The ones who quit sometimes do it for reasons that, if properly understood and considered, can lead them to return. But that takes boldness and courage.'

I pick up on what the Holy Father is saying, and refer to the fact that there are Christians who live in situations that are not regular in the light of the Church, or in complex situations – Christians who, in one way or another, live open wounds. I am thinking of those who have divorced and remarried, homosexual couples, other difficult situations. How can we reach out pastorally to such people? What tools should we use? The Pope indicates that he has understood my question and replies.

'We need to proclaim the Gospel on every street corner,' the Pope says, 'preaching the good news of the Kingdom of God, and healing, even with our preaching, every kind of disease and wound. In Buenos Aires, I used to receive letters from homosexual people who are "socially wounded" because they tell me that they feel as if the Church has always condemned them. But the Church does not want to do this. During the return flight from Rio de Janeiro I said that if a homosexual person is of good will and is in search of God, I am no one to judge. By saying this, I said precisely what the *Catechism* says. Religion has the right to express its opinion in the service of the people, but God with His creation has set us free: it is not possible to interfere spiritually in the life of a person.'

'A person once asked me, as if to be provocative, if I approved of homosexuality. I replied with another question: "Tell me: when God looks at a gay person, does he affectionately approve of this person's existence, or does he reject the person with condemnation?" We must always consider the person. Here we enter into the mystery of the human being. In life, God accompanies people, and we must accompany them, starting from their particular situation. It is necessary to accompany them with mercy. When that happens, the Holy Spirit inspires the priest to say the right thing.'

'This is also the beauty of Confession: evaluating each case individually and being able to discern what is the best thing to do for a person who seeks God and his grace. The confessional is not a torture chamber, but the place in which the Lord's mercy motivates us to do better. My thoughts turn to the situation of a woman who carries the burden of a failed marriage in which she had had an abortion. Then this woman remarries, and is now happy with five children. That abortion weighs heavily on her conscience and she sincerely regrets it. She would like to move forward in her Christian life. What is the confessor to do?'

'We cannot dwell only on issues related to abortion, gay marriage and the use of contraceptive methods. This is not possible. I have not spoken much about these things, and I have been reprimanded for that. But when we speak about these issues, we have to talk about them in a context. The position of the Church, for that matter, is known, and I am a son of the Church, and therefore it is unnecessary to talk about these issues all the time.'

'The dogmatic and moral teachings of the Church are not all equivalent. The Church's pastoral ministry cannot be obsessed with the transmission of a disjointed multitude of doctrines to be imposed insistently. Proclamation in a missionary style focuses on the essentials, on the necessary things: this is also what fascinates, and is a more attractive proposition, what makes the heart burn, as it did for the disciples at Emmaus. We have to find a new balance; otherwise the moral edifice of the Church is likely to fall like a house of cards, and risk losing the Gospel's freshness and fragrance. The Gospel's proposal must be simpler, profounder, more radiant. It is from this proposition that the moral consequences then flow.'

'I say this also thinking about preaching and the content of our preaching. A beautiful homily, a genuine homily must begin with the first proclamation, with the proclamation of salvation. There is nothing more solid, deep and sure than this proclamation. Then you have to do catechesis. Then you can also draw a moral consequence. But the proclamation of the saving love of God comes before moral and religious imperatives. Today, sometimes it seems that the opposite approach is prevailing.

The homily is the touchstone to measure the pastor's proximity and ability to meet his people, because those who preach must recognize the heart of their community and must be able to see where the desire for God is alive and ardent. The message of the Gospel, therefore, is not to be reduced to certain aspects that, although relevant on their own, do not go to the heart of the message of Jesus Christ.'

The first Pope from a religious order in 182 years...

Pope Francis is the first Pontiff to come from a religious order since the Camaldolese Gregory XVI, elected in 1831, 182 years ago. So I ask: 'What is the specific place of religious men and women in the eyes of the Church?'

'The religious are prophets', says the Pope. 'They are those who have chosen to follow Jesus, and imitate his life in obedience to the Father, to poverty, to community life and to chastity. In this sense, the vows cannot become caricatures; otherwise, for example, community life becomes hell, and chastity becomes a way of life for unfruitful bachelors. The vow of chastity must be a vow of fruitfulness. In the Church, the religious are called to be prophets, in particular, by demonstrating how Jesus lived on this earth, and to proclaim how the Kingdom of God will be in its perfection. A religious must never give up prophesizing.'

'This does not mean opposing the hierarchy of the Church, although the prophetic function and the hierarchical structure do not coincide. I am talking about a proposal which is always positive, but that should not be timid. Let us think about what so many great saints, monks and religious men and women have done, from St Anthony the Abbot onward. Being prophets may sometimes involve making *ruido* [Spanish for noise]. I do not know how to put it... Prophecy makes noise, uproar, some say "a mess". But in reality, the charism of religious people is like yeast: prophecy announces the spirit of the Gospel.'

The Roman dicasteries, synodality and ecumenism

Following up on his reference to the hierarchy, I ask the Pope: 'What do you think of the Roman dicasteries?'

'The Roman dicasteries are at the service of the Pope and the bishops', he says. 'They should help both individual Churches and the bishops' conferences. They are instruments of help. In some cases, however, when they are not functioning effectively, they run the risk of becoming institutions of censorship. It is striking to see the number of reports of a lack of orthodoxy which are sent to Rome. I think each case should be investigated by the local bishops' conferences, which can rely on valuable assistance from Rome. These cases, in fact, are much better dealt with locally. The Roman dicasteries are mediators; they are not middlemen or managers.'

I remind the Pope that on 29 June 2013, during the ceremony of the blessing and imposition of the pallium on thirty-four metropolitan archbishops, he had affirmed 'the path of synodality' as the path that leads the united Church to 'grow in harmony with the service of the primate'. So I ask: 'How can we harmoniously reconcile the Petrine primacy with synodality? Which roads are feasible, not least from an ecumenical perspective?'

'We must walk together: the people, the bishops and the Pope. Synodality is lived at various levels. Maybe it is time to change the methods of the Synod, because it seems to me that the current method is not dynamic. This can also have ecumenical value, especially with our Orthodox brethren. From them we can learn more about the meaning of episcopal collegiality and the tradition of synodality.'

The joint effort of reflection, looking at how the Church was governed in the early centuries, before the division between East and West, will bear fruit in due time. In ecumenical relations it is important not only to know each other better, but also to recognize what the Spirit has sown in the other as a gift for us too. I want to continue the discussion which commenced in 2007 between the joint [Catholic–Orthodox] commission on how to exercise the Petrine primacy, which led to the signing of the Ravenna Document. We must continue along this path.

I want to understand how the Pope envisions the future of the unity of the Church. He replies: 'We must walk united with our differences: there is no other way to become one. This is the way of Jesus.'

And what about the role of women in the Church? The Pope has referred several times to this subject on various occasions. In one interview he affirmed that the feminine presence in the Church has not sufficiently emerged, because the temptation of male chauvinism has left no room to ensure that the role due to women is visible in the community.

He addressed the issue again on his flight back from Rio de Janeiro, claiming that the Church has not yet achieved a profound theology of women. So I ask: 'What should the role of women in the Church be? What can we do to make their role more visible today?'

'It is necessary to make more room for a more incisive feminine presence in the Church. I am wary of a solution that can be reduced to a kind of "machismo in a frock", because a woman has a different make-up to that of a man. But what I hear about the role of women is often inspired by an ideology of machismo. Women are asking important questions that must be addressed. The Church cannot be herself without women playing their role. Women are essential for the Church.'

'Mary, a woman, is more important than the bishops. I say this because we must not confuse function with dignity. We must, therefore, investigate the role of women in the Church further. We have to work harder to develop a profound theology of woman. Only by taking this step will it be possible to reflect better on women's function within the Church. The feminine genius is needed wherever we make important decisions. The challenge today is this: to think about the specific role of women precisely where the authority of the Church is exercised in various areas of the Church.'

The Second Vatican Council

'What did the Second Vatican Council accomplish? What was it?' I ask in the light of his preceding statements, imagining a long and articulate response. Instead I have the impression that the Pope simply considers the Council to be a fact not open for discussion, about which it is not worth talking at length, so as to reconfirm its importance.

'Vatican II was a re-reading of the Gospel in light of contemporary culture. It produced a renewal movement that simply originates from the same Gospel. Its fruits are enormous. Just recall the liturgy. The work of liturgical reform has been a service to the people as a re-reading of the Gospel from a concrete historical situation. Yes, there are herme-neutics of continuity and discontinuity, but one thing is clear: the dynamic of reading the Gospel, actual-izing its message in today's world – which was typical of the Council – is absolutely irreversible. Then there are particular issues, like the liturgy according to the *Vetus Ordo*. I think the decision of Pope Benedict was prudent and motivated by the desire to help people who have this sensitivity. What is worrying, though, is the risk of the ideologization of the *Vetus Ordo*, its exploitation.'

The Church – a field hospital

Since the very first moments of his Petrine ministry, Pope Francis has proposed as the image of the Church that of the people of God travelling 'in the light of the Lord' (Isa. 2.5). One need only think of his words immediately after his election to the pontificate: 'And now, let us embark on the journey: bishop and people', he had said. 'Now I would like to give the blessing, but first, first, I ask you a favour: before the bishop blesses the people, I ask you to pray to the Lord that he may bless me: the prayer of the people, asking blessing for their bishop.'

With this call for prayer, the Pope took those people who at that moment saw themselves as bowing to receive a blessing, and turned them into 'actors' and protagonists. By his actions, the Pope likes to turn the people before him into actors. Or at least invite them to act. In fact, rather than 'communicating', Pope Francis creates 'communicative events', in which those who receive his message are active participants. 'God enters that popular dynamic.' The Church for Bergoglio, as for de Lubac who inspires him, has nothing to do with the idea of an invisible, restricted society of a small number of elect.

The vital dynamic of the Church, as set out during the Mass pro Ecclesia celebrated with the Cardinal Electors in the Sistine Chapel on 14 March, is to 'Walk, build, confess'. We need only remember that St Ignatius of Loyola refers to the 'physical exercise' of walking as a way of understanding the 'spiritual exercise' (SE, 3). The Church, on a 'spiritual and missionary journey', is called to 'build itself on the cornerstone that is the Lord himself', confessing its faith in him. The holiness that the Pope loves and feels close to is the 'middle', common holiness that expresses both great patience and great constancy in its day-to-day walk. The 'icons' of that holiness are his grandmother Rosa, the nurse who saved his life, the old priest who looks back on his life of service. This 'middle class of holiness' is not in fact mediocre: on the contrary, it is the one capable of being fruitful and generative. For the Pope, fruitfulness is the characteristic trait of a life worth living. But what does that 'fruitfulness' mean for the Church?

A reply emerges from the Pope's words: the portrait of a Church capable of approaching every man and walking side by side with him, like Jesus with his disciples in Emmaus: 'Jesus himself came up and walked along with them' (Lk. 24.15). As has seemed clear, however, walking with man does not actually mean adapting to the spirit of the world. Bergoglio violently resists the 'spiritual worldiness' that precedes that ethic. He sees the traps of individualism, of relativism, of secularism. Walking with someone means neither adapting nor yielding, but supporting.

Pope Francis's pontificate is profoundly 'dramatic'. Bergoglio's is a militant reading of reality, in conflict with worldliness and with the demon evoked several times in his speeches. But evoking the demon means that people cannot be demonized. Evil, sin, temptation are very clear. The Church of Pope Francis is a Church in discernment that lives with its eyes open in constant attentiveness to God, able to read events with realism, to be alert to that which surrounds it. And discernment, still according to the Ignatian tradition, must be guided by the 'consolation' which, according to Ignatius of Loyola, 'inflames the soul' (SE, 316) and warms the heart. And this is Bergoglio's appeal: 'Are we still a Church capable of warming the heart? A Church capable of leading us back to Jerusalem? Of walking us home?'

Company, listening, warmth, versus distance, cold, rigidity, hence: 'We need a Church that will bring warmth again, that will warm the heart'.[1] This is the fruitful Church, capable of giving life to the world.

**

The closeness that the Church must demonstrate to man is concretely manifested in the Pope's attitude: in the 'unusual' phone calls to people who have written to him, in his choice to be among people, and in his officials' desperate fears about his security, as happened during his trip to Brazil for World Youth Day at the end of July 2013.

The Pope himself talked about this to journalists: 'Security here, security there; there wasn't a single accident in the whole of Rio de Janeiro during these days, and everything was spontaneous. With less security, I could have been with the people, I could have embraced them, greeted them, without armoured cars... there is security in trusting a people. It is true that there is always the danger of some mad person. The danger that some mad person will do something, but then there is the Lord! But to make an armed space between the bishop and the people is madness, and I prefer the other madness: away with it! And run the risk of the other madness! I prefer this madness: away with it! Closeness is good for us all.'[2]

In an earlier interview with Gerson Camarotti of the Brazilian channel Rede Globo, the Pope, again answering a question about his security, had been even clearer about his motivations: 'If you go and see someone you really love, friends, with a desire to communicate, are you going to see them in a glass box? No. I couldn't go and see these people, with such big hearts, behind a glass box. And in the car, when I drive down the street, I lower the window so that I can put my hand out and wave. So it's all or nothing: either you travel as you must, or you don't; half communication is no good.' And he concluded: 'Because I come and visit people, I want to treat them like people. Touch them.'[3]

In the same interview the Pope traces the roots of this fruitful attitude, without physical barriers, to the motherhood of the Church: 'What is fundamental for me is the closeness of the Church. The Church is a mother, and mothers don't communicate "by correspondence". A mother gives affection, touch, kisses, love. When the Church, busy with a thousand things, neglects closeness, it forgets about it and only communicates in written documents, it's like a mother communicating with her son by letter.' Several times in the past, the then Cardinal Bergoglio had spoken of the 'maternal warmth' of the Church.[4] And this warmth is also manifested physically. For Bergoglio that requires the logic of the Incarnation. So anyone who sees the Pope's gesture as an expression of simple naïveté has not really understood what is happening, its profound significance.

His need to be close to people – above all those in difficulties, the poor, the marginalized – has manifested itself many times. We might remember the visit to Lampedusa, his words on his visits to Cagliari or in Brazil, in some extremely symbolic places. In Varghinha, a well-known favela in Rio de Janeiro, the Pope expressed his desire for closeness like this: 'It is wonderful to be here with you! It is wonderful! From the start, my wish in planning this visit to Brazil was to be able to visit every district throughout the nation. I would have liked to knock on every door, to say "good morning", to ask for a glass of cold water, to take a cafezinho – not a glass of grappa! – to speak as one would to family friends, to listen to each person pouring out his or her heart – parents, children, grandparents

… But Brazil is so vast! It is impossible to knock on every door! So I chose to come here, to visit your community, this community, which today stands for every district in Brazil. How wonderful it is to be welcomed with such love, generosity, and joy!'[5]

This is evangelical joy. At the hospital of São Francisco de Assis na Providência, everyone saw the warm embraces between the Pope and former drug addicts. There he exclaimed: 'Embrace, embrace. We all need to learn to embrace those in need, as St Francis did.'[6] To knock at the door of the heart you therefore need to have 'bare' hands, to have no filters, to touch the flesh. For Pope Francis this physical dimension is not an accessory, a mere question of 'style', but part of the communication of the strong message of the Incarnation.

The paradigm for this ability to communicate is the parable of the good Samaritan (Lk. 10.29–35), and the reference to the 'Samaritan Church' is already present in the founding document of Aparecida, produced by the Fifth Episcopal Conference of Latin America held in the Brazilian city in 2007, in which Cardinal Bergoglio played a central role. In this document the Church is presented as the vehicle of consolation and joy, the means of direct encounter with the Lord: 'Life in Christ includes the joy of eating together, enthusiasm for making progress, the pleasure of working and learning, the joy of serving whoever needs us, contact with nature, enthusiasm for communal projects, the pleasure of living sexuality in keeping with the Gospel, and all the things that the Father gives us as signs of his sincere love. We can find the Lord in the midst of the joys of our limited existence, and that gives rise to sincere gratitude. So the mercy of the "Samaritan Church" tends to cure the wounds of those who feel rejected or excluded so that man can live this happy, whole, full life, a "life in abundance"' (no. 356).

But the deep roots of the 'Samaritan Church' lie in the address of Paul VI, a pontiff greatly loved by Francis, on the occasion of the final public session of Vatican II, when he said: 'The old story of the Samaritan has been the model of the spirituality of the council.' These are words to which Pope Francis would fully subscribe.

**

At the heart of my discussion with Pope Francis an image emerges: that of the Church as a 'field hospital after a battle'. It is a very potent image, which also contains within it the dramatic perception of a world living in warlike conditions with deaths and injuries. In his morning homily at Santa Marta on 22 October 2013, Pope Francis elaborated on this metaphor. 'The image that comes to my mind is that of a nurse in a hospital who heals our wounds, one at a time. Just like God, who gets involved and meddles in our miseries, He gets close to our wounds and heals them with His hands. And to actually have hands, He became man. It is a personal work of Jesus. A man made sin, a man comes to cure it. Closeness. God doesn't save just because of a decree, a law; he saves us with tenderness, he saves us with caresses, he saves us with his life, for us.'

The weakness of the human condition is the starting point for the mission that must above all consider to whom the message of salvation should be addressed. If the Church has before it a wounded man who needs salvation, it cannot and must not proceed to measure his cholesterol or glycaemia, it has to save his life, it has to bring him the message of salvation. This cannot be reduced to 'little precepts'. Here the Pope is not in fact playing down the moral teachings of the Church, as has been suggested. Rather he is distinguishing the indispensable from what comes next. And the indispensable must be easily comprehensible.

The problem becomes apparent when the message conveyed by the Church is identified with aspects that do not inwardly manifest the heart of the message itself. In short, the Pope is inviting us to put the moral teaching of the Church inside the context that gives it meaning. It is a stage in the missionary conversion, both pastoral and spiritual, of the Church. In fact, for Bergoglio, all of the Church's activity should be seen from a missionary perspective. For Bergoglio, the Church exists not to talk about itself nor to be talked about, but to announce the God of Jesus Christ, to talk about him to the world and with the world.

In particular, the ministry of the Gospel is above all a ministry of mercy which 'washes, cleans, relieves'. It should be pointed out that this work of succour and salvation does not consider the 'wounded man' as entirely deprived of a capacity to react, as simply a dying man, in short.

The images that Bergoglio draws from the world of medicine should be elaborated with care. For the Pope, 'a sick person cannot be cured if we don't start from what is healthy about him'.[7] And that means starting from the positive, from those resources which are still available, from an undamaged openness to Grace, from health that has not been incurably undermined. I have always found myself thinking about an event in Pope Francis's life which I have always connected with the attitude of 'cure', not least in the medical sense, which he frequently expresses: the fact that before entering the seminary Bergoglio fell seriously ill and at the age of 21 suffered a near-fatal lung infection. In a moment of high fever he embraced his mother, saying desperately: 'Tell me what's happening to me!'[8] He was diagnosed with pneumonia and the presence of three cysts. As a result the upper part of his right lung was amputated.

His convalescence was difficult because of the method of aspirating the fluid that formed in his lungs. I imagine what it might mean to a young man to be short of breath and be in need of immediate treatment, of relief. I think that in some way this marked the great and profound human and spiritual sensibility of Pope Francis. One question that the Pope asked vibrantly during our conversation was: 'How are we treating the people of God?' It's a central question, one that he poses every day, even before worrying about structures which are also important. And the word 'treat' should perhaps be read in the sense of 'cure' in the context of a 'field hospital'.

**

The Church that Bergoglio has in mind is above all the 'Mother and Shepherdess' who generates and accompanies, taking on the burden of others on the basis of their concrete existential condition. 'We must always consider the person', the Pope says to me. 'Here we enter into the mystery of the human being.' The realm of consciousness is a sacred realm because it is the place where the human being meets

God. For Bergoglio the mission is characterized by radical openness to the action of God within every human being. Especially in a time of crisis such as ours, belonging to the Church is a process of growth in a profound relationship that arises out of the condition of light or shade lived by each one of us.

Besides, the roots of this vision of the Church made up of pardoned and chosen sinners, Samaritan and merciful to the utmost, are one more way of seeking, among other things, in the formation of Francis, linked to the Ignatian tradition of seeking the will of God over the single individual to whom God communicates in person. It is the perspective of the Spiritual Exercises of St Ignatius of Loyola, which has always at its centre the person trying to open themselves up to the will of God over their life. When the Pope talks of what he calls 'spiritual management', this is precisely what he means: the Church must freely express its own thought, and must do so in dialogue with a personal freedom that demands to be respected, precisely because the truth of Christianity is in dialogue with a kind of freedom.

In his letter to Eugenio Scalfari, published in *La Repubblica* of 11 September 2013, the Pope writes: 'To start, I would not speak about, not even for those who believe, an "absolute" truth, in the sense that absolute is something detached, something lacking any relationship. Now, the truth is a relationship! This is so true that each of us sees the truth and expresses it, starting from oneself: from one's history and culture, from the situation in which one lives, etc. This does not mean that the truth is variable and subjective. It means that it is given to us only as a way and a life.'

We must understand these words carefully: rather than insisting, in fact, on an objective norm beyond discussion, to which individual Christians themselves must conform, Pope Francis's perspective prefers to remain open to the Spirit which speaks to the believer through life, in the originality of the situations that the believer lives in the present, in the heart of a historical moment and in the community of believers that is the Church.

The truth of God 'is inexhaustible, it is an ocean whose shore we can barely see. It is something that we are beginning to discover in these times: let us not make ourselves slaves to an almost paranoid defence of our truth (if I have it, he hasn't got it; if he can have it, it means that I can't have it). The truth is a gift that is broad for us, and precisely for that reason it broadens us, amplifies us, elevates us. And it places us at the service of that gift.'[9]

Bergoglio speaks of the 'beauty' and 'explosiveness'[10] (*belleza y explosividad*) of this truth. Education into the truth of God is therefore a crucial task. Bergoglio stressed this years ago when he spoke of Christian schools, which are not called 'to train a hegemonic army of Christians who will know all the answers. They should be the place in which questions are received, where, in the light of the Gospel, a personal quest is encouraged, not interrupted with walls of words, walls that are rather weak and collapse after a short time.'[11]

**

As Bergoglio will say later in our interview, 'you never know where, and how, you will find [God]. You cannot set the time and place of your encounter with Him.' In this context the message of the Church, therefore including its moral message, is never separate from pastoral concerns, from the welfare of the person to whom it is addressed: hence it is always 'relative'.

In the interview the Pope states explicitly: 'We cannot dwell only on issues related to abortion, gay marriage and the use of contraceptive methods.' On the question of same-sex marriage, 'the Church already has a clear position', the Pope has stated, but that is not to say that we face a limit in terms of the Gospel or the way to meet the Lord. When, on his return flight from Rio de Janeiro, the Pope said 'If a person is gay and seeks God and has good will, who am I to judge him?', he was suggesting a different way of facing the question, more closely connected to accompaniment along the road, to the personal encounter between God and man. Later in the interview he would say: 'You must, therefore, discern the encounter.' This is an important point: you must discern not only the presence of God, but also the encounter, where and how it happens. That is the focus of the question: the relationship with God of a person who is searching for him. So there are no taboos – and even homosexuality must not and cannot be taboo – but there are borders that the Church is called upon to inhabit as it spreads the Gospel.

Key to Bergoglio's interests is kerygma, the spreading of the Christian message, while, he told me, he fears a pastoral ministry 'obsessed with the transmission of a disjointed multitude of doctrines to be imposed insistently'. In the past he has lamented the fact that sermons 'prefer to speak of sexual morality and everything connected with sex. You can do this, you can't do this. This is wrong, this is not. And then we end up forgetting the treasure of the living Jesus, the treasure of the Holy Spirit present in our hears, the treasure of a project of Christian life that has many implications which go far beyond mere sexual questions. We ignore a very rich catechesis, with the mysteries of faith, the credo, and end up concentrating on whether or not to take part in a demonstration against a planned law in favour of the use of contraceptives.'[12]

Pope Francis's fear is that priorities will be lost, and that we will see the 'beauty of kerygma degraded to a grim sexual morality'.[13] The problem, then, as he says in the interview, is that the 'moral edifice of the Church is likely to fall like a house of cards'. He had already spoken of it in his brief homily at Mass with the cardinals in the Sistine Chapel the day after his election, when he said: 'What happens is what happens to children on the beach when they make sandcastles: everything collapses, it is without consistency.'

He had previously spoken of 'walls that are rather weak and collapse after a short time'.[14] In this sense I believe that the call of Jesus to Francis of Assisi, 'go, repair my house', resonates strongly in the Pope's soul. He is not only concerned with the external cracks, but with the lack of solidity in the kerygmatic proclamation.

**

And the proclamation of the Gospel also requires an opening of doors. Precisely because the heart of its mission is closeness, the doors of Pope Francis's Church are always open: open to let people in and open to let the Gospel into the world, without locking it up inside internal fortifications.

On 17 October 2013, in his homily at morning Mass at Santa Marta, the Pontiff commented on the Gospel passage from Luke (11.47–54) that records the admonition of Jesus to the doctors of the law: 'Woe to you, because you build tombs for the prophets, and it was your ancestors who killed them.' With this he associated the image of 'a closed Church' into which 'the people passing by cannot enter', and from which 'the Lord inside cannot leave'.

Hence his call to those 'Christians who have the key in their hand, but take it away, without opening the door'; or worse, 'keep the door closed' and 'don't let anyone in'. In the Christian who assumes 'this attitude of "keeping the key in his pocket, with the door closed"' there is, according to the Pope, 'an entire spiritual and mental process' which leads to putting faith 'through a distiller' and transforming it into 'ideology'.

But the 'ideology', he warned, 'does not summon. There is no Jesus in ideologies. Jesus is tenderness, love, meekness, and ideologies, of whatever hue, are always rigid.' So much so that they risk making the Christian 'the disciple of this attitude of thought' rather than a 'disciple of Jesus'.

Obviously it would be wrong and naïve to identify 'ideology' with 'culture'. Pope Francis maintains that inculturation is part of the process of the 'incarnation' of the Christian message in a specific context. The Gospel undergoes chemical changes, becoming an ideology at the moment when one seeks to restrict its immediate power to a cultural, social or political context. The Gospel must be a source of its own hermeneutics. Any other approach, in fact, 'enslaves' the Gospel; it does not 'serve' it.

So Christ's reproach remains relevant: 'You have taken away the key of knowledge', because 'the knowledge of Jesus is transformed into an ideological and also a moralistic knowledge', following the behaviour of those same doctors of the law who 'closed the door with many prescriptions'.

The Pope has also referred to another warning from Christ – the one contained in Chapter 23 of the Gospel of Matthew – against scribes and Pharisees who 'tie heavy burdens and place them on people's shoulders'. It is precisely because of these attitudes, in fact, that a process begins through which 'faith becomes ideology and ideology frightens! Ideology chases people away and distances the Church from the people.'

In his Letter to the Archdiocese of Buenos Aires for the Year of Faith, the then Cardinal Bergoglio had loudly lamented the fact that 'Growing insecurity has been leading people, little by little, to lock the doors, to install safety devices and security cameras, to distrust the stranger who calls at the door.'[15]

For Bergoglio, the closed door seems to be a symbol of the contemporary world which refers to a lifestyle, a way of facing reality, of facing others, of facing the future. In fact, 'The image of an open door has always been the symbol of light, friendship, joy, freedom, confidence. How we need to recover these things! The closed door harms us, paralyzes us, separates us.'[16]

The theme of 'open doors' is central to Pope Francis's preaching, which calls for a Church that is not preoccupied with fortifying its confines, but seeking encounter. This is the radical missionary spirit that I have seen vividly in dialogue with Pope Francis. So it isn't enough to open doors: we must go into the streets, even if it means running risks. 'I need to go into the street, to be with people', he told me at one point, when we were talking about his home at Santa Marta.

Let us remember that these very thoughts accompanied Bergoglio at the Conclave from which he would emerge Bishop of Rome. In fact, among the key points of his intervention during the General Congregation meetings, then handed over to

Cardinal Ortega (and broadcast by him by prior agreement), we read: 'Rather than being just a Church that welcomes and receives, we try to be a Church that goes out to the world, and goes towards the men and women who do not attend it, who do not know it, who have not been to it, who are indifferent.'[17]

During the trip to Brazil, addressing bishops, priests, religious and seminarians in the homily of the Mass dedicated to them in Rio Cathedral on 27 July, the Pope sought to stress that the pastoral ministry cannot be reduced to encounters and plans that he had defined some time ago as 'cough syrup',[18] but that what is required is fidelity to Christ and a radical leaving of the protected places of the faith.

In one heartfelt passage, Francis, talking about the education of the young, affirmed: 'Let us form them in mission, to go out, to go forth, to be itinerants who communicate the faith. Jesus did this with his own disciples: he did not keep them under his wing like a hen with her chicks. He sent them out! We cannot keep ourselves shut up in parishes, in our communities, in our parish or diocesan institutions, when so many people are waiting for the Gospel! To go out as ones sent.

'It is not enough simply to open the door in welcome

because they come, but we must go out through that door to seek and meet the people! Let us urge our young people to go forth. Of course, they will make mistakes, but let us not be afraid! The Apostles made mistakes before us. Let us urge them to go forth. Let us think resolutely about pastoral needs, beginning on the outskirts, with those who are farthest away, with those who do not usually go to church. They are the VIPs who are invited. Go and search for them at the crossroads.'[19]

The term 'existential peripheries' is one of Pope Francis's best-known. The invitation is motivated not least by the fact that for Pope Francis, reality is perceived 'better from the periphery than from the centre'.[20] Being on the periphery helps us to see and understand things better, to make a more correct analysis of reality, escaping centralism and ideological approaches. For this reason, among other things, in the interview he placed a great deal of stress on the Church's need not to close itself away 'in pastoral laboratories', but to live and think in the midst of reality.

** **

A missionary Church is a Church that goes into the street to proclaim the announcement of salvation, an announcement that 'makes the heart burn'. For that reason the reference to the episode of the disciples of Emmaus in the last chapter of Luke's Gospel (24.13–35) is central: it is an episode particularly dear to Pope Francis, who again suggested it in his recent meeting with the Brazilian bishops.

The two disciples escape from Jerusalem, scandalized by the failure of the Messiah in whom they had believed. Here we can read the difficult mystery of people who leave the Church; the mystery, that is, of many who maintain that it can no longer offer anything meaningful or important. Why? The Pope makes a synthetic but profound analysis of the reasons of those who remove themselves from the Church: 'Perhaps the Church appeared too weak, perhaps too distant from their needs, perhaps too poor to respond to their concerns, perhaps too cold, perhaps too caught up with itself, perhaps a prisoner of its own rigid formulas; perhaps the world seems to have made the Church a relic of the past, unfit for new questions; perhaps the Church could speak to people in their infancy but not to those come of age.'[21]

This list of 'perhaps' is in reality a list of sins or, at least, temptations that the Church experiences on its way through history, and which are summed up in an attitude of distance, coldness, rigidity. It prompts an examination of the conscience of the Church. Faced with this situation, what are we to do? Which

Church would the human beings of today, like the two disciples of Emmaus, need?

The Pope, then, sets out a truly vivid, positive portrait of the Church, accompanying it with an analysis of the condition of contemporary man: 'We need a Church unafraid of going forth into their night. We need a Church capable of meeting them on their way. We need a Church capable of entering into their conversation. We need a Church able to dialogue with those disciples who, having left Jerusalem behind, are wandering aimlessly, alone, with their own disappointment, disillusioned by a Christianity now considered barren, fruitless soil, incapable of generating meaning.'[22]

That dialogue is also needed if we wish to understand the reasons for someone leaving: 'The ones who quit sometimes do it for reasons that, if properly understood and considered, can lead them to return.' Here the Pope is stressing the positive, good desire that lies in every human being, and that can even lead them to make choices which, as in this case, might be seen as wrong. But within the wrong decision there sometimes lies a sound motivation.

For example, if someone has quit the Church because his subjective experience is negative or one of inauthenticity, the desire for authenticity may be capable of bringing him back to the bosom of the Church. The Pope also told me that accompanying the herd also means trusting the fact that the herd 'can detect the scent of new roads'.

At one point he talked to me about the 'sense of smell of faith'. For Bergoglio, as for Ignatius of Loyola, the senses are both physical and spiritual. The spiritual senses are those involved in discernment. And the Church on the road is a Church in discernment that finds the road together, following the 'scent' of faith. And that certainly implies decentralization. Discernment concerns the Church as a whole, and many problematic areas have a territorial dimension. It should therefore be expected that the role of the local bishops will be optimized.

Pope Francis wants the Church to be salt and light, that is, a 'lighthouse' that illuminates from a high and stable position, but also 'flickers', that can move amid people, accompanying them on their treacherous journey, whatever direction it may take, to ensure that for many the light does not remain only a distant memory.

**

When we move on to talk about the ecclesiastical structures, the bonds that unite Pope Francis's

Church, which is on a spiritual journey and builds itself by confessing Christ, are powerful bonds. Certainly for him, as clearly emerges from the interview, the Church is always the people with its pastors. The hierarchy seen in isolation, within itself, he said to me in passing, has never fascinated him, but he has always been fascinated by the Church as a totality of the people of God. In this vision everything assumes form and beauty.

When it came to talking to his 'fellow cardinals', immediately after his election, Pope Francis used very precise and clear expressions to define the type of bond that unites the College, which gave me a more general understanding of what it means to him to live in an 'intense ecclesiastical communion': he has spoken of 'reciprocal knowledge of one another and mutual openness', of 'that community, that friendship, that closeness, that will do good for every one of us', of 'authentic collegial affection', of 'fraternally sharing our feelings, experiences and reflections'.[23]

Pope Francis seeks to experience an affectionate and effective collegiality. Let us not forget that Benedict XVI, in his last speeches as Pope, insisted on the Church as a living body that must also mould service structures. The Curia, for example, must be the expression not of 'an excogitated, theoretically constructed insitution', but a 'living reality', according to the words of Romano Guardini that Benedict XVI recalled in his farewell to the Cardinals.

The Church is the universal Ecclesia, a reality with a geographical extent that covers the whole world. The universal breath must mould it intimately, not least because the most vital and dynamic ecclesial experiences are happening in the younger Churches. Benedict XVI gave the College of Cardinals a very beautiful image: that of 'an orchestra, in which diversities – the expression of the universal Church – always contribute to a higher and concordant harmony'. Alongside the diversity of sounds, what arises today is the question of their intensity and the playing of the instruments. Pope Francis picked up his predecessor's musical images in his general audience on 9 October 2013, defining the Church as the 'house of harmony'.

These, then, are the challenges to the exercise of the primacy; synodality, episcopal collegiality, ecumenism. Anyone interested in understanding the fundamental elements of the reform that Pope Francis has in mind will already have deduced some key points from the interview: Bergoglio knows how to wait as long as necessary, he likes to take decisions at the right moment, he knows how to trust his collaborators, he wants real rather than formal consultations, he wants to grant space to collegiality by lowering the level of centralization, he appreciates shared decisions. At any rate, I believe that the most important thing for Bergoglio is not the simplification of the structure of the Curia, but the development of participation within the Church.

In the course of my dialogue with him, Pope Francis's affective 'afflatus' appeared intensely when we touched upon the ecumenical challenge. From his first gestures and his first words, the Pope has shown that he wants to take as his starting point the 1995 encyclical *Ut unum sint*, in which John Paul II affirmed that he felt called to 'find a way of exercising the primacy which, while in no way renouncing what is essential to its mission, is nonetheless open to a new situation' and thus, taking up the words addressed to the Ecumenical Patriarch Demetrius I of Constantinople on 6 December 1987, invoked: 'I insistently pray the Holy Spirit to shine his light upon us, enlightening all the Pastors and theologians of our Churches, that we may seek – together, of course – the forms in which this ministry may accomplish a service of love recognized by all concerned' (no. 95).

One effect was concretely manifested in the fact that, for the first time since the schism of 1054, an Orthodox Patriarch, Bartholomew I, took part in the inaugural Mass of a pontificate. The Pope's 'afflatus' would also have an impact on inter-religious dialogue, as was demonstrated by the sending of a telegram by the Pope to the Chief Rabbi of Rome on the day of his election, and then on the occasion of the Jewish Passover. It is in this sense that we should re-read the speech delivered during the audience to the representatives of the Churches, of the ecclesiastic Communities, and other religions on 20 March in the Sala Clementina. There he called Bartholomew 'my brother Andrew' (in fact, just as the Bishop of Rome is the successor to Peter, the Patriarch of Constantinople descends from the apostle Andrew, Peter's brother); there he said he had seen 'in some way prefigured' the 'full realization' of unity among believers in Christ; there he expressed the 'firm will to continue along the path of ecumenical dialogue'.

To place such stress on relations of communion – not least in their perceptible, sensible dimension – means relying on reciprocal trust to overcome pessimism and discouragement, 'so that the star of hope may shine brightly'. So here we see the emergence of a later challenge to the pontificate of Pope Francis – a wide-ranging challenge.

**

But in fact, for Pope Francis, the gift and the challenge of the communion that the Church lives within itself concerns the whole of society. The Church, he wrote some time ago, 'exhorts us to share that which makes us different, or the charism of each one of us, the personal belonging of each of us to groups, political parties, non-governmental organizations, parishes, different circles'.[24] Learning to share differences is the premise for politics to transcend the fluctuating, provisional balance of interests, because 'to be a citizen means being called to make a change, called to a struggle, to this struggle of belonging to a society and a people'.[25]

For Bergoglio, belonging has a very high value, both ecclesiastic and civil. And the laicity of the state, the reciprocal autonomy of Church and State, their horizontal and equal relationship, guarantee citizenship as a 'collective work in constant construction',[26] in which the things that make us different should be put in common, including political or religious affiliations.

In this sense, on the other hand, Bergoglio fully espouses the Augustinian critique of a religion understood as an 'essential part of the whole symbolic and imaginary construction' that sustains 'society through a sacralized power'.[27] Political reality is never the Reign of God on earth. In Pope Francis's broad vision of the Church in itself and its relationship with the world, Vatican II remains an inescapable point of reference. Pope Francis's proposition is 'prophetic' in the sense in which Yves

Congar used the term, referring to one who 'confers to the movement of time its true relationship with God's design'.[28]

In this sense Francis is a Pope of the Council – not in the sense that he repeats it, constantly quotes and defends it, but in the sense that he takes up its intimate value as a 'dynamic of the reading of the Gospel, actualizing its message in today's world', of a 're-reading of the Gospel in the light of contemporary culture', as he affirmed in the course of our interview. But he also said to me: 'Now we need to go forward.'

Seeking and finding God in all things

Pope Francis's discourse is very much focused on the challenges of today's world. Years ago he wrote that in order to see reality one must have a gaze of faith, otherwise one sees reality in pieces, fragmented. This is also one of the themes of the encyclical *Lumen fidei*. I am also thinking of certain passages in the speeches of Pope Francis during World Youth Day in Rio de Janeiro. I quote them to him: 'God is real and manifests himself in the present day'; 'God is everywhere'. They are phrases that echo Ignatius's expression, 'to seek and find God in all things'. So I ask the Pope: 'Your Holiness, how does one seek and find God in all things?'

He replies: 'What I said in Rio referred to the time in which we seek God. In fact, there is a temptation to seek God in the past, or in a possible future. God is certainly in the past because we can see the footprints of His presence. And God is also in the future as a promise. But the 'concrete' God, so to speak, is today. For this reason, complaining never, never helps us find God. The complaints of today about how "barbaric" the world is – these complaints sometimes end up founding within the Church the desire to establish order in the sense of pure conservation, as a defence. No: God is to be encountered in the world of today.

'God manifests himself in historical revelation, in history. Time initiates processes, and space crystallizes them. God is in history, in the processes under way. We must not focus on occupying the spaces where power is exercised, but rather on starting long-run [long-term] historical processes. We must initiate processes rather than occupy spaces. God manifests himself in time and is present in the processes of history. This gives priority to actions that give birth to new historical dynamics. And it requires patience; waiting.

'Finding God in all things is not an "empirical *eureka*". Deep down, when we desire to encounter God, we would like to verify him immediately by an empirical method. But we cannot meet God this way. God is found in the gentle breeze perceived by Elijah. The senses that find God are the ones St Ignatius called spiritual senses. Ignatius asks us to open our spiritual sensitivity to encounter God beyond a purely empirical approach. A contemplative attitude is necessary: it is the feeling that we are moving along the good path of understanding and affection toward things and situations. Profound peace, spiritual consolation, love of God and seeing all things in God – this is the sign that you are on this right path.'

Certitude and mistakes

'If the encounter with God in all things is not an "empirical *eureka*",' I ask the Pope, 'and if it is therefore a journey that reads history, mistakes can also be made...'

'Yes, in this quest to seek and find God in all things there is always an area of uncertainty. There must be. If a person says that he has met God with total certainty and is not touched by a margin of uncertainty, then this is not good. For me, this is an important turning point. Claiming to have the answers to all the questions is proof that God is not with a person. It means that he is a false prophet using religion for personal gain. The great leaders of the people of God, like Moses, always left room for doubt. You must leave room for the Lord, not for our certainties; we must be humble. Uncertainty is in every true discernment which is open to finding confirmation in spiritual consolation.'

'The risk in seeking and finding God in all things, then, is the willingness to explain too much; to say with human certainty and arrogance, "God is here". We will find only a God who is made-to-measure. The correct approach is that of St Augustine: seek God to find him, and find God to keep on searching

97

for God forever. Often we seek by groping about, as one reads in the Bible. And this is the experience of the great fathers of the faith, who are our models. We have to re-read the Letter to the Hebrews, Chapter 11. Abraham leaves his home without knowing where he is going, by faith is he guided. All of our ancestors in the faith died in their struggle to seeing the good that was promised them, but from a distance… Our life is not given to us like an opera libretto, in which everything is written down; but it means going, walking, doing, searching, seeing… We must enter into the adventure of the quest to meet God; we must let God search and encounter us.

'Because God is first; God is always first and makes the first move. God is a bit like the almond flower of your Sicily, Antonio, which always blooms first. We read it in the Prophets. God is encountered while travelling along our path. At this juncture, someone might say that this is relativism. Is it relativism? Yes, if it is misunderstood as a kind of indistinct pantheism. It is not relativism if it is understood in the biblical sense, that God is always a surprise, so you never know where, and how, you will find Him. You cannot set the time and place of your encounter with Him. You must, therefore, discern the encounter. Discernment is essential.'

'If the Christian is a restorationist, a legalist, if he wants everything clear and safe, then he will find nothing. Tradition and memory of the past helps us to have the courage to open up new areas to God. Those who today always look for disciplinarian solutions, those who long for exaggerated doctrinal "security", those who stubbornly try to recover a past that no longer exists – they have a static and inward-directed view of things.'

In this way, faith becomes an ideology among other ideologies. I have a dogmatic certainty: God is in every person's life. God is in everyone's life. Even if the life of a person has been a disaster, even if it is destroyed by vices, drugs or anything else – God is in that person's life. You can and must try to seek God in every human life. Although the life of a person is a land full of thorns and weeds, there is always a space in which the good seed can grow. You have to trust God.'

Do we have to be optimistic?

These words of the Pope's remind me of some of his past reflections, in which the then Cardinal Bergoglio wrote that God is already living in the city, vigorously mixed in the midst of all and united to each. It is another way, in my opinion, to say what St Ignatius wrote in the Spiritual Exercises: God 'labours and works' in our world. So I ask: 'Do we have to be optimistic? What are the signs of hope in today's world? How can I be optimistic in a world in crisis?'

99

'I do not like to use the word optimism because it refers to a psychological state', the Pope says. 'I prefer to use the word hope instead, according to what we read in the Letter to the Hebrews, Chapter 11, which I have mentioned before. The Fathers kept walking, overcoming great hardships. And hope does not disappoint, as we read in the Letter to the Romans. Think instead of the first riddle of Puccini's opera *Turandot*', the Pope suggests. At that moment I recall, more or less by heart, the verses of the riddle of the princes in *Turandot*, to which the solution is hope: 'In the gloomy night flies an iridescent ghost./ It rises and opens its wings / on the infinite black humanity. / The whole world invokes it / and the whole world implores it. / But the ghost disappears with the dawn / to be reborn in the heart. / And every night it is born / and every day it dies!' Verses that reveal the desire for a hope that here is merely an iridescent ghost that disappears with the dawn.

'You see,' Pope Francis continues, 'Christian hope is not a ghost and it does not deceive. It is a theological virtue and therefore, ultimately, a gift from God that cannot be reduced to optimism, which is only human. God does not mislead hope; God cannot deny himself. God is all promise.'

A spirituality for our time

For Bergoglio, the reading of the Gospel in history and in the light of contemporary culture means that God manifests himself in the present day, and that human history should be considered as 'the place of discernment among offers of Grace'.[1] It is not far either from the lives of individuals or from history and its processes. Pope Francis ponders this vision in the practice of the Spiritual Exercises, in which Ignatius of Loyola asks us to 'look how God dwells in creatures: in the elements, giving them being, in the animals feeling in them, in men giving them to understand; and so in me, giving me being, animating me, giving me sensation and making me to understand; likewise making a temple of me, being created to the likeness and image of His Divine Majesty' (SE, 235).

And then he asks us to consider the action of God: 'Consider how God labours and works for me in all things created on the face of the earth, that is, behaves like one that labours – as in the elements, plants, fruits, cattle, etc., giving them being, preserving them, giving them vegetation and sensation, etc.' (SE, 236).

If the idea is to 'seek God in all things', in this dynamic process mission and change are guided either by faithfulness to the Gospel and to the Spirit, or by changes that are recorded in the world. On this the Pope is clear: 'God is everywhere: we have to know how to find Him in order to be able to proclaim Him in the language of each and every culture; every reality, every language, has its own rhythm.' Alongside the spiritual vision of great trust in the presence of God in the world, we realize that Bergoglio's perspective is rooted in the existential questions of the people of today, and particularly those of the rising generations. So we have to 'seek' God. But 'finding him' is not, for Bergoglio, an empirical *eureka*. God is not an object that falls in front of our eyes, which our capacity for knowledge can possess. What is required is a contemplative attitude which recognizes His presence through the profound peace that He gives. This certitude says much about the Bergoglian vision of the world. It is a dynamic vision, lively but static. He also talked to me about four principles of his vision: 'Time is superior to space, superior to conflict, reality is superior to the idea, the whole is superior to the part.'

He is particularly attached to the first of these principles. Time indicates cultural, social, spiritual processes, while space indicates fixed, precise places for us to be or to occupy. For Christians, it is a matter of 'starting processes, more than occupying spaces', he said to me. Basically, the Gospel image of the yeast that ferments the dough is the icon of a process in action.[2]

But so is the image of the wheat and the weeds, which cannot grow together. Here the temptation would be to eradicate the weeds straight away. In fact, however, 'the sower's eye must be filled with hope. When he sees the weeds sprouting amidst the wheat, he does not react by lamenting or causing alarm, but trusts in the fertility of the seed, overcoming the temptation to speed up time'.[3] The wheat and the weeds will grow together, then, but we are called to protect to the grain, leaving the harvesting of the weeds to the angels.[4]

His vision is not excessively rooted in doctrinal 'certitude', but is very alert and focused upon processes in action. Pope Francis says clearly in the interview that God manifests himself in time and is present in the processes of history, which 'presses upon us and often leaves us breathless'.[5] And we are called to a 'humble assumption of the burden of reality, of history, of the promise'[6] of God. This privileges the actions that generate new dynamics, and perhaps also new ways of living the relationship with God: 'If we stay only within the parameters of "culture as it has always been", basically a culture with a rural basis, the final result will be the annihilation of the force of the Holy Spirit.'[7] For Bergoglio, Providence offers us new possibilities: a crisis is also a challenge.[8]

Here Pope Francis is pointing towards a radical task: the reconstruction of the imagination of faith in a changing society, in which symbolic and cultural references are no longer what they once were. The very view that man has of himself, he says to me, 'changes over time, and so even man's consciousness deepens'. And this process also includes 'the dogma of the Christian religion, consolidating over the years, developing over time, deepening with age', as we read in the Commonitorium Primum of St Vincent of Lérins, which the Pope would later quote to me.

During the homily at the Easter Vigil of 2013, shortly after his election, Pope Francis had insisted on one aspect that establishes a mentality open to permanent reform: newness. He said: 'Doesn't the same thing also happen to us when something completely new occurs in our everyday life? We stop short, we don't understand, we don't know what to do. *Newness* often makes us fearful.'

The Pope gives us a lesson in life, and urges the Church to be open, radically willing to receive even that which does not correspond to the mental categories that we have formed over time. Bergoglio wrote in a truly glowing passage: 'Any closed, definitive discourse always conceals many perils; it hides that which must not come to light, it tries to gag the truth which is always open to that which is truly definitive, something that is not part of this world.'[9]

What must fall are false ideas of tradition and conversation: 'Staying, remaining faithful implies an exit. Precisely if we remain within the Lord, we leave ourselves. Paradoxically, in fact, because we remain, precisely if we are faithful, we change. We don't remain faithful, like traditionalists or fundamentalists, to the letter. Faithfulness is always a change, a flourishing, a growth. The Lord works a change in anyone who is faithful to him.'[10] The Christian, Pope Francis tells me, 'cannot live in panic or live on consolidated certitudes'.

In his letter to the diocese for the opening of the Year of Faith, Cardinal Bergoglio had written of the necessity to 'accompany the continuous movement of life and history without falling into the paralysing defeatism according to which the past is always better than the present'. He urges us to think the new, to bring the new, to create the new, kneading life with the new yeast of justice and sanctity (1 Cor. 5–8).[11]

Living in history means living in possibility, because the human story 'is never over, it never exhausts its possibilities, but can always open itself up to the new, to that which had not been taken into acount until now. To that which seemed impossible. Because that history is part of a creation whose roots lie in the Power and Love of God.'[12]

**

But looking for God in the new also means being constantly available to let oneself be found by the Lord, given that it is He who seeks us. This is the true contemplative attitude. And therein lies salvation, as Cardinal Bergoglio wrote in his preface to a book about St Augustine: 'There is the point: some believe that faith and salvation come with our effort to look for, to seek the Lord. Whereas it's the opposite: you are saved when the Lord looks for you, when He looks at you and you let yourself be looked at and sought for. The Lord will look for you first. And when you find Him, you understand that He was waiting there looking at you, He was expecting you from beforehand. That is salvation: He loves you *beforehand*. And you let yourself be loved. Salvation is precisely this meeting where He works first.'[13]

Bergoglio loves the existential position of Augustine in search of God, and says so clearly during the interview: 'The correct attitude is the Augustinian one: seeking God to find him, and finding him to seek him for ever.' When the Pope said these words to me, he had recently celebrated Mass for the start of the General Chapter of the Order of St Augustine, on 28 August 2013. There he had spoken of the 'peace of disquiet'. Bergoglio's relationship with God, his personal experience of God, cannot disregard this disquiet, knowing however that God seeks us first. A person who received a personal note from Pope Francis read me this phrase with great emotion: 'God seeks us, God waits for us, God finds us... before we seek him, before we wait for him, before we find him. That is the mystery of holiness.'

Even in his discussion with Rabbi Skorka, Bergoglio confessed: 'I would say that we find God while walking, strolling, seeking Him and being sought by Him. These are two roads meeting. On the one hand, we seek him driven by an instinct born in our hearts. And then, when we encounter one another, we realize that He was already looking for us, that he had been ahead of us.'[14]

God comes first, he is ahead of us. This is also the meaning of the slang word *primerear* used by Pope Francis. He explained to me that it is not a good or innocuous word. It can mean taking the initiative first or before the other person realizes, but the connotation is negative because it substantially means taking the initiative before the other person realizes and cheating, tricking them. Pope Francis used the expression even during the Pentecost Vigil before the Ecclesial Movements on 18 May 2013. This time he referred to God himself: 'We say we must seek God, go to Him and ask forgiveness, but when we go, He is waiting for us, He is there first! In Spanish we have a word that explains this well: *primerear* – the Lord always gets there before us, he gets there first, he is waiting for us. You go to him as a sinner, but he is waiting to forgive you. The Lord is waiting for us. Moreover, when we seek him, we discover that he is waiting to welcome us, to offer us his love. And this fills your heart with such wonder that you can hardly believe it, and this is how your faith grows. Some people will say, "No, I prefer to read about faith in books!" It is important to read about faith, but look, on its own this is not enough! What is important is our encounter with Jesus, our encounter with him, and this is what gives you faith because he is the one who gives it to you!'

Hence 'the spiritual experience of the encounter with God is not controllable'.[15] The God of Bergoglio is also the *Deus semper maior* of St Ignatius of Loyola, the 'God of surprises'. 'God is creative, he is not closed, so he is never rigid. God is not rigid!' Pope Francis said in a speech to the Catechists on 27 September 2013. So our lives must not rigidify. Human life is not an already written score, an 'opera libretto', says Bergoglio. There is a dimension of uncertainty, of incompleteness, that is an integral part of a life of faith which is, he says in the interview, 'adventure', 'quest', the opening up of new spaces to God.

One of the characteristics of Pope Bergoglio, which is also revealed in this interview, is his very driving existential position. But Bergoglio prefers not to be defined as an 'optimist'. He has always been a realist, not bound to aprioristic visions of trust in the progressive destinies of humanity. His optimism in reality is faith, evangelical trust that gives shape to a way of seeing reality. It is the fruit of creativity seen as 'active hope'.[16]

This is the attitude lived by the Latin American episcopate at Aparecida in 2007, embodied in the method 'see, judge, act' (no. 19). 'Seeing', in fact, is not simple empirical observation, but 'the contemplation of God with the eyes of faith', so that we can 'see the reality that surrounds us in the light of His providence'. The 'optimism' for Bergoglio, who does not give in to the perception of being 'defeated', arises out of this 'vision' of faith.

IV

Art and creativity

I am struck by the quotation from *Turandot* to explain the mystery of hope. I would like to have a better understanding of Pope Francis's artistic and literary references. I remind him that in 2006 he had said that the great artists are able to present the tragic and painful realities of life with beauty. So I ask him who his favourite artists and writers are, and if they have anything in common...

'I have really loved a diverse array of authors. I love Dostoevsky and Hölderlin very much. I remember Hölderlin for that very beautiful poem written for his grandmother's birthday; it was spiritually very enriching for me. The poem ends with the line, "*May the man hold fast to what the child has promised*". I was also struck by it because I loved my grandmother Rosa, and in the poem, Hölderlin compares his grandmother to the Virgin Mary, who gave birth to Jesus, the friend of the earth who did not consider anybody a foreigner.'

'I have read *The Betrothed* [by Alessandro Manzoni] three times, and I have it now on my table because I want to read it again. Manzoni has given me very much. When I was a child, my grandmother read it to me, and I learnt the beginning by heart: "That branch of Lake Como that turns off to the south between two unbroken chains of mountains…" I also like Gerard Manley Hopkins very much.

'Among painters, I admire Caravaggio; his paintings speak to me. But also Chagall, with his "White Crucifixion". Among musicians I love Mozart, of course. The *Et incarnatus est* from his *Mass in C minor* is without parallel; it lifts you to God! I love Mozart performed by Clara Haskil. Mozart fulfils me: I cannot think about his music; I have to listen to it. I like listening to Beethoven, but in a Promethean way, and the most Promethean interpreter for me is Furtwängler.

And then Bach's *Passions*. The piece by Bach which I love the most is the *Erbarme Dich*, the tears of Peter in the *St Matthew Passion*. Sublime. Then, on a different level, not on a personal level in the same way, I love Wagner. I like to listen to him, but not all the time. The performance of Wagner's *Ring* by Furtwängler at La Scala in Milan in 1950 is for me the best. But also the *Parsifal* by Knappertsbusch in 1962.

'We should also talk about cinema. *La Strada*, by Fellini, is the movie which perhaps I loved the most. I identify with this movie, in which there is an implicit reference to St Francis. I also believe that I watched all of the movies with Anna Magnani and

Aldo Fabrizi when I was between 10 and 12 years old. Another film I loved was *Rome, Open City*. I owe my film culture to my parents especially who used to take us to the movies quite often.

'Anyway, in general I love tragic artists, especially classical ones. There is a nice definition that Cervantes's character, the bachelor Carrasco, gives to praise the story of Don Quixote: "Children have it in their hands, young people read it, adults understand it, the elderly praise it." For me this is a good definition of the classics.'

I realize that I am transfixed by these references, and that I want to enter into his life through the door of his artistic choices. This might be a long trip: it would include cinema, from Italian neorealism to *Babette's Feast*. Other authors and works come to my mind to which he has referred on other occasions, including minor, less well-known or local ones: from *Martin Fierro* by José Hernández to the poetry of Nino Cosa, to *Il Grande Esodo* by Luigi Orsenigo. I also think of Joseph Malègue and José María Pemán. And clearly also of Dante and Borges, but also of Leopoldo Marechal, the author of *Adán Buenosayres*, *El Banquete de Severo Arcángelo* and *Megafón o la Guerra*.

I think in particular of Borges because Bergoglio, while just a 20-year-old working as a teacher of literature in Santa Fé at the *Colegio de la Inmaculada Concepción*, had direct contact with him. Bergoglio taught students in the last two years of the secondary school and directed his students toward creative writing. I had a similar experience to his when I was his age, at the Istituto Massimo of Rome, where I founded BombaCarta; I talk with him about it, and ask the Pope to describe his experiences.

'It was a bit risky', he answers. 'I had to make sure that my students studied *El Cid*. But the boys did not like it, they wanted to read García Lorca. Then I decided that they would study *El Cid* at home and that in class I would base my lessons on the authors the boys preferred. Of course, those young students wanted to read racier literary works, like the contemporary *La Casada Infiel* by García Lorca, or classics like *La Celestina* by Fernando de Rojas. But by reading these things they acquired a taste for literature, poetry, and we went on to read other authors. And that was a great experience for me.

'I completed the programme, but in an unstructured way – that is, not in the order according to what we expected at the beginning, but in an order that flowed naturally from reading these authors. And this method befitted me: I did not like to have a rigid schedule, but rather, I liked to know where we were going with the readings, with a rough sense of where we were headed. Then I also got them to write, and in concluding the course I decided to send two of the stories written by my students to Borges. I knew his secretary, who had been my piano teacher. And Borges liked the stories very much. And then he wrote the introduction to a collection of these students' writings.'

'Therefore, Holy Father, creativity is important for the life of a person?' I ask. He laughs and replies: 'For a Jesuit it is extremely important! A Jesuit must be creative.'

Frontiers and laboratories

Creativity, therefore, is important for a Jesuit. During a visit by the fathers and collaborators of *La Civiltà Cattolica*, the Pope identified a triad of other important characteristics of the cultural work of Jesuits. That day, 14 June, comes to mind, and I remember that, in the talk prior to the meeting with the whole group, he outlined the triad: dialogue; discernment; frontier. And he insisted particularly on the last point, citing Paul VI and what he had said in a famous speech about the Jesuits: 'Wherever in the Church – even in the most difficult and extreme fields, in the crossroads of ideologies, in the social trenches – there has been and is now conversation between the deepest desires of human beings and the perennial message of the Gospel; Jesuits have been there, and are there still.'

I ask Pope Francis to clarify a few points. 'You have asked us to be careful not to fall to [into] the "temptation of taming the frontier: we should move toward the frontier, but not take the frontier home to trivialize it and tame it". To what were you referring? What exactly are you saying to us? This interview was co-coordinated by a group of journals published by the Society of Jesus: what invitation do you wish to extend to them? What should their priorities be?'

'The three key words that I commended to *La Civiltà Cattolica* can be extended to all the journals of the Society, perhaps with different emphases according to their formats and their goals. When I insist on the frontier, I am referring in a particular way to the need for those who work in the world of culture to be embedded into the context in which they operate and on which they reflect. There is always the lurking danger of living in a laboratory. Ours is not a "lab faith" but a "journey faith", a historical faith. God has revealed himself as history, not as a compendium of abstract truths. I am afraid of laboratories because the problems are taken to the laboratory, and then taken home so as to be tamed, to paint them out of their context. You cannot bring the frontier home, but you have to live on the border and be bold.'

I ask the Pope for examples from his personal experience. 'When it comes to social issues, it is one thing to hold a meeting to discuss the problem of drugs in a slum neighbourhood, and quite another thing to go there, live there and understand the problem from the inside and study it. There is a brilliant letter by Father Arrupe to the Centres for Social Research and Action on poverty, in which he says clearly that one cannot speak of poverty if one does not experience poverty, with a direct connection to the places in which there is poverty. The word *insertion* here is dangerous, because some religious have interpreted this as being a fad, and disasters have occurred because of a lack of discernment. But it is truly important.

'The frontiers are many; let us think of the nuns living in hospitals. They live on the frontier. I am alive thanks to one of them. When I was admitted to hospital because of lung disease, the doctor gave me penicillin and streptomycin in specific doses. The sister who was on duty tripled my doses of these medicines because she sensed that something was wrong; she knew what to do because she spent her days and nights among the sick patients. The extremely competent doctor lived in his laboratory; however, the sister lived on the frontier and was in constant dialogue with it every day. Domesticating the frontier means just referring to it from a remote location, locking oneself up in a laboratory. Laboratories are useful, but reflection for us must always start from experience.'

Human self-understanding

I then ask the Pope if this is also true for the important cultural frontier of the challenge of anthropology, and if so, how. The anthropology which the Church has traditionally used and the language with which it has expressed it remain a solid point of reference – the fruit of secular wisdom and experience. Nevertheless the people to whom the Church is turning do not seem to understand it, or they consider it insufficient. I begin to think about the fact that people are interpreting themselves differently from the past, by using different categories. This is partly due to the major changes in society and to a broader study of themselves.

At this moment, the Pope gets up and walks over to his desk to get his breviary. It is in Latin, well worn from use. He opens it to the Office of Readings for Friday of the 27th Week in Ordinary Time and reads me a passage from the *Commonitorium Primum* of St Vincent of Lérins: *ita étiam christiánae religiónis dogma sequátur has decet proféctuum leges, ut annis scílicet consolidétur, dilatétur témpore, sublimétur aetáte* ['Even the dogma of the Christian religion must follow these laws, consolidating over the years, developing over time, deepening with age'].

The Pope comments: 'St Vincent of Lérins makes a comparison between the biological development of man and the transmission from one era to another of the *depositum fidei* [deposit of faith], which grows and is strengthened with time. Here, human self-understanding changes with time and, with it, does human consciousness deepen. Let us think of when slavery was considered acceptable, or the death penalty was applied without question. So we grow in the understanding of the truth. Exegetes and theologians help the Church to mature in her own judgement. The other sciences and their development also help the Church in its growth in understanding. There are secondary ecclesiastical rules and precepts that were once effective, but now they have lost their value and meaning. The view of the Church's teaching as a monolith to defend without nuance or different understandings is wrong.

'After all, in every age of history, humans have tried to understand and express themselves better. So human beings in time change the way they perceive themselves. It's one thing for a man who expresses himself by carving the *Nike* [Winged Victory of Samothrace], yet another for Caravaggio, Chagall, and yet another still for Dalí. The forms for expressing truth can likewise be multiform, and this is indeed necessary for the transmission of the Gospel in its timeless meaning.'

'Humans are in search of themselves, and of course, in seeking, they can make mistakes. The Church

119

has experienced times of brilliance, like that of Thomism. But the Church has also lived through times when it experienced a decline in its ability to think. For example, we must not confuse the genius of Thomism with that of decadent Thomism. Unfortunately, I studied philosophy from textbooks which came from decadent Thomism. Therefore, in thinking of the human being the Church should strive for genius and not for decadence.

'When does a formulated thought cease to be valid? When it loses sight of the human, or even when it is afraid of the human or deluded about itself. The depiction of the deceived thought is like Odysseus's encounter with the song of the Siren, or like Tannhäuser in an orgy surrounded by satyrs and bacchantes, or like Parsifal, in the second act of Wagner's opera, in the palace of Klingsor. The thinking of the Church must recover genius and a better understanding how human beings understand themselves today, in order to develop and deepen the Church's teaching.'

We have to be creative

When the Pope explained hope to me by quoting the riddle from Puccini's *Turandot*, I admit I was thrown off guard. I wasn't even sure that I had understood correctly, and asked him to repeat what he had just started saying. Then I realized something that has subsequently been confirmed to me. Bergoglio is not just a learned person, he is someone who experiences art and creative expression as a dimension that is an integral part of his spirituality and his pastoral ministry.

A number of times before, while hearing the Pope speak, I had caught a quoted passage put there without any preamble or learned explanation. I remember, for example, the quotation of the *Impatient Divine* by José María Pemán during his homily to the Jesuits for the feast of St Ignatius in the Church of the Gesù on 31 July 2013. Likewise, the reference to Malègue in the interview, when he spoke of the 'middle class of holiness'. For Bergoglio, art is an integral part of life and of discourse on life. It is not a world apart, scholarly, learned, lofty. His radically 'popular' vision also applies to artistic production. I don't think he has ever dedicated a separate speech to the subject.

So art is to be considered as part of his discourse on man, on spirituality, on pastoral ministry and the mission of the Church. Literature, in particular, teaches us to compare words with life. In this regard it is useful to note the reference to *The Betrothed* in the interview.

The Pope has implicitly quoted this novel, which at the time of the interview he had on his desk, when, addressing the Ecclesial Movements at the Pentecost

Vigil, he wrote: 'It's not so much about speaking, but about speaking with our whole lives.' In particular, here he is quoting the chapter he loves the best, the one about the conversion of the Nameless One, where we read: 'Life is the touchstone of words.'

This is the point: life is the touchstone of words. The novel speaks of Federigo Borromeo for whom, Manzoni writes, 'there is no right superiority of man over men, save in their service'. This chapter in *The Betrothed*, in which the character of Cardinal Federigo is described in his encounter with the Nameless One, should be examined further if we wish to find elements of Bergoglio's vision. Let us also recall that Paul VI quoted the same passage in his general audience on 9 October 1968.

Another moment in the interview which convinced me of this is when the Pope tells me that the forms of expression of truth can be manifold, and that in fact man changes his way of perceiving himself over time. Bergoglio does not resort to more sophisti- cated reflect- ions about anthropological change, but says that one thing is the Hellenistic image of man that produced the *Nike* of Samothrace, and another that finds its forms in the paintings of Caravaggio, and yet another that of Dalí's Surrealism.

So if we wish to understand the Pope's relationship

with art the citations of Odysseus, *Tannhäuser* and *Parsifal* are very useful when it comes to speaking of the thoughts that delude humankind, and the need for the Church to recover its 'genius' in the understanding of life and human experience. I'm enormously impressed by this appeal to genius, which the Pope contrasts with the decadence of sterile thought.

I was also very struck by the moment when the Pope told me that he loves Mozart performed by Clara Haskil: 'It fills me up: I can't think it, I have to feel it', he affirmed to me in a meditative voice. Those few words contain a whole conception of the aesthetic enjoyment that disintguishes 'feeling' and 'thinking'. We taste an artist through feeling rather than thought, not that the former excludes the latter. But it is possible that feeling is so strong, rich and involving as to overcome any theoretical analysis.

Bergoglio wrote in 2005: 'Wisdom doesn't stop at knowledge. Knowing also means tasting. We know knowledge... and we also know flavours.'[1] You have to understand that behind this kind of aesthetic outline on Bergoglio's part there is a passage from Ignatius's Spiritual Exercises, in which he says, right at the beginning: 'For it is not knowing much, but feeling and relishing things inwardly, that contents and satisfies the soul' (SE, 2). And for Bergoglio 'feeling', in one way or another, always has something to do with the manifestation of God in the soul and in a person's life. It is the thought of Ignatius, and the thought of Peter Faber that Pope Francis likes so much.

**

This is not the place to dwell on the Pope's favourite artists, or the works that have most marked him. Still, the one constant seems to be the sense of the tragic. He repeated this to me several times during our discussion. But it is not an elite, refined tragedy; it is 'popular' tragedy – so much so that he takes his definition of a 'classic' work from Cervantes: 'Children have it in their hands, young people read it, adults understand it, the elderly praise it.' The 'classic' work is the one that everyone can somehow feel as their own, not something that belongs to a small group of refined connoisseurs. The passion for neorealism should be inserted into this vision of art that has a connection with the people. Just as the interest in a work that Bergoglio likes even if it is not in fact, by his own admission, a masterpiece: the epic Argentinean poem *Martin Fierro*, written by José Hernández in 1872, which gives form to a society in which everyone has a place: 'The *porteño* businessman, the coastal gaucho, the shepherd from the North, the craftsman from the North East, the aborigine and the immigrant, to the extent that none of them wishes to have everything for himself, expelling the other from the earth.'[2] These words recall the democratic, popular romanticism of a poet like Walt Whitman, a contemporary of Hernández, who brings onstage the carpenter from Dakota or the Californian miner, the mechanic and the bricklayer, the boatman and the cobbler.[3]

So it is interesting to note how the popular dynamic of Bergoglio's aesthetic is the same as his pastoral and ecclesiological vision. Art is not a 'laboratory' for experiments in cultural and expressive dynamics: in fact it is part of the flux of history, part of man's journey on earth. If anything it is an advance frontier, but not an elite circle. We have to be creative and brilliant, the Pope insists, but the genius and the creative person do not live in isolation: creating art and cultivating beauty belong to the community, not the individual.[4]

I think that this vision of the aesthetic experience helped the Pope during his experience as a teacher of literature, of which he speaks in this interview. Bergoglio was a teacher of literature and psychology at the *Colegio de la Inmaculada Concepción* in the Argentinean city of Santa Fé in 1964–5. He was twenty-eight at the time.

His students called him *carucha*, 'the looker', 'angel-face', as we might say. But they recognized that behind that face there was a methodical man who wanted to get the best out of them. Recalling his pupils of those intense years, in 2005 Bergoglio wrote: 'They were my psychology and literature pupils in years IV and V of *liceo classico*. They were lively, creative boys. The literary exercise that I asked them to do was to write stories; I was impressed by their narrative abilities. I selected some of the stories they had written and showed them to Borges. He too was struck by their work, and encouraged the publication of their stories; he also wanted to write a preface to the edition himself. Can we say that they were little geniuses? I wouldn't go that far; I'm sure they were perfectly normal.' And he concludes: 'I also want to express my wish that their lives make history beyond the personal history of each one of them. That they make history by inspiring many young people along a creative path.'[5]

Why and how did these young people open themselves up so passionately to creative writing? Above all, I believe, because young Mr Bergoglio is convinced that poetry is the 'test' of the dignity and greatness of the individual, as he clearly said during his interview with Sergio Rubin and Francesca Ambrogetti: 'Man continues to show altruistic behaviour, to write beautiful things, to make poetry, to paint, to invent new technologies and to make advances in science.'[6] He must have communicated that to his students.

But in Bergoglio's pedagogical experience we also

find an interesting, if 'risky', criterion, as he himself admits, to reflect upon. His young pupils didn't want to study the classics and asked to read authors closer to their sensibility, but also closer to their curiosity. Young Mr Bergoglio realized that he was tilting at windmills. In the end he decided that it was only by addressing their immediate tastes that he would help these boys to enter the world of writing and literature. And that was what he did.

Bergoglio followed his own inclination not to follow too rigid a programme. But above all he understood that it was only by making them write that he would be able to make them understand the experience of writing, but from within. His pupils began to write, and their stories were read by Borges, with whom they formed a close relationship. The case in question is a happy application of some principles that guide Bergoglio both in his pastoral ministry and in the mission of the Church: the precise perception of context; attention to the people he is addressing and their demands; the need to accompany them and turn them into actors, protagonists.

**

During our conversation the Pope also made various references to the journal that I've edited since 2011, *La Civiltà Cattolica*. It's the oldest cultural journal to have been published in Italy without interruption. Written entirely by Jesuits, it is particularly attuned to the Pope and the Apostolic See. We both remembered the audience that he gave three months after his election, on 14 June 2013. On that occasion he had given us some precise indications about how we should proceed, and how to define our cultural work. He summed it up in three words: dialogue, discernment, frontier. In this conversation he repeated those three words and extended their validity to all the journals of the Society of Jesus. In reality the impression is that these three words are 'key' to him in all cultural work carried out by Christians.

The first word was 'dialogue': dialogue has a meaning only if we recognize in those before us an interlocutor who has something good to say. Without falling into relativism, we have to make room for different points of view, often supported not only by individuals, but also by cultural, social and political institutions, to understand their reasons from within. The task of a cultural journal like ours, then, can not be purely eulogistic, but must include the effort to understand the deep reasons of cultural, political and social debates. Without understanding, one cannot reflect or help others – readers – to understand. In a time like ours, in which supporting one's own positions often means delegitimizing the others who think differently, the Pope's invitation to design a serious and effective cultural approach becomes all the more urgent and valid.

The second word was 'discernment'. A cultural initiative must immerse itself in the world to listen to its pulsing heart, to recognize its desires, its expectations and frustrations, and the presence of God's work in it. On 16 March, three days after his election, the Pope had told the media: 'You have the ability to gather and express the expectations and needs of our time, to provide the elements for a reading of reality.' But with particular reference to *La Civiltà Cattolica* he said : 'With humble and open intelligence, "seek and find God in all things", as St Ignatius wrote. God is at work in the life of every man and in the culture: the Spirit blows where it will. Seek to discover what God has operated and how His work will proceed.'

The third word was 'frontier'. In the audience before his meeting with the other Jesuits on the editorial board, the Pope had told me in advance that he would exhort us in particular not to fall into the temptation of 'domesticating' frontiers: 'you have to go towards frontiers and not bring the frontiers home to paint them up a little and tame them', he said to us. The Church is called to live at the frontiers to be really in contact with every human reality, even the most remote. The objective is not the annexation of frontiers, but our ability to live in difficult areas and come into contact with 'remote' cultural and social realities that have not yet been reached by the word of the Gospel. In our interview, he later stressed that even those engaged in cultural work cannot live a 'laboratory' dynamic. The Pope fears laboratories because in them problems are not lived in their context, but are abstract and tamed. For him, study and reflection can be valid only if they do not anticipate direct integration, direct participation in the cultural dynamics that are being studied and reflected upon. Hence there is no reflection without experience.

V

Prayer

I ask the Pope one last question about his preferred way of praying.

'I pray the Breviary every morning, I like to pray with the psalms. Following that, I celebrate Mass. I pray the Rosary. What I really like is adoration in the evening, even when I am distracted and think of other things, or even fall asleep praying. In the evening then, between seven and eight o'clock, I spend an hour in front of the Blessed Sacrament in adoration. But I pray mentally even when I am waiting at the dentist, or at other times of the day.

'Prayer for me is always full of memory, of recollection, even the memory of my own history, or of what the Lord has done in his Church or in a particular parish. For me, it is the memory of which St Ignatius speaks in the First Week of the *Exercises* in the merciful encounter with Christ crucified. And I ask myself: "What have I done for Christ? What am I doing for Christ? What should I do for Christ?" It is the memory of which Ignatius speaks in the *Contemplatio ad amorem* [Contemplation for Loving like God,] when he asks us to recall the gifts we have received. But above all, I also know that the Lord remembers me. I can forget about him, but I know that he never, ever forgets me. Memory has a fundamental role for the heart of a Jesuit: the memory of grace, the memory spoken of in Deuteronomy, the memory of God's works that are the basis of the covenant between God and the people. It is this memory that makes me his son and which makes me a father, too.'

**

At this moment, though realizing I would like to continue with our dialogue, I recall the Pope once saying we must not 'abuse the limits'.

All told, we had spoken for more than six hours over our three encounters in August (19, 23 and 29). Here, I have presented our conversation without indicating the breaks between each encounter in order to maintain continuity. We had more of a conversation than an interview; the questions served as a foundation, and did not impede the conversation with predetermined rigid parameters. Linguistically, we moved seamlessly between Italian and Spanish without incurring unnecessary pauses – in fact, we hardly noticed as we moved from one to the other. Nothing was mechanical, and the answers sprang forth spontaneously from the dialogue and from a reasoning which here I have tried to express syntheti-cally, as best I am able.

The foundation: Prayer

I take my leave of the Pope by broaching a topic that acts as a pedestal to our whole dialogue: prayer. During our whole conversation I had a sense that I was talking to someone immersed in God, capable of profound peace. This is not to take anything away from the Pope's passion, but in fact acts as a foundation for it, giving it density and direction.

Bergoglio is at once volcanic and serene. I perceive that this internal condition is rooted in prayer. In 2007, in a letter to his priests, he wrote: we do not pray in order to 'be comfortable with our conscience, or in order to enjoy a purely aesthetic internal harmony. When we pray we are fighting for our people.'[1] This is a little like what Moses did at Refidim against Amalek: fighting while holding his hands raised to heaven in prayer (Exod. 17.8–13). Contemplation and action inter-penetrate, as Ignatius of Loyola claimed, *in actione contemplativus.*

The fundamental traits of his prayer are simple: he would call them 'normal'. They are those of any priest. He prays with his breviary, a book in Latin now worn by use, and prays 'mentally', in a silent inner dialogue with God. He loves the prayer that accompanies life and its moments, just as he enjoys silent worship, in which he sometimes dozes off.

In the past he dwelt upon that silent worship that has been part of his life for a long time: 'I feel as if I were in someone else's hands, as if God were holding me by the hand.'[2] I was struck that he said he prayed 'when I'm waiting at the dentist'. He didn't say 'when I was waiting', but used the present tense: 'I'm waiting'. I smiled to myself: clearly the Pope hasn't yet got used to the idea of a life without standing in queues, without waiting... But that little open window on his daily life is certainly striking.

Pope Francis's prayer has its own setting in ordinary life, and its typical characteristic is to be 'memorioso' – 'full of memory' – as he himself says in a neologism. Bergoglio contemplates experience, history, the life lived by him and the life lived by others and by the Church. And he turns this into memory and is grateful for it. He likes to call to mind the blessings he has received, to make remembrance Grace. In a reflection on education, Bergoglio wrote: 'Making remembrance, in the Biblical sense, goes beyond mere thanks for what we have received; it means teaching ourselves to feel more love; it seeks to confirm us in the journey we have undertaken. Memory as thanks for the presence of the Lord on our path through life. The memory of the past that guides us, not as a useless burden, but as a fact interpreted in the light of present awareness.'[3]

An example of this prayer 'filled with memory' is the fact that Pope Francis keeps in his breviary the spiritual testament of his grandmother Rosa, which is, for him, a prayer. In it we read among other things: 'That these grandchildren of mine, to whom I have dedicated the best of myself, may have a long, happy life. But if one day pain, illness or the loss of a dear one should fill them with affliction, let them always remember that a sigh at the Tabernacle, where the greatest and most noble martyr is kept, and a glance at Mary at the foot of the cross, can cause a drop of balm to fall on the deepest and most painful wounds.'[4]

For the Pope, prayer is not detached from real life, from dear ones, from history: it is never 'absolute', but always 'relative' to situations, to contexts. The extreme concreteness and 'fleshliness', I might say, of his prayer, is provided by Chapter 16 of the Book of the Prophet Ezekiel. I discover, in fact, in my conversation with the Pope once the microphones are turned off, that he particularly likes this passage. He recognizes himself in that chapter. It was another big surprise in my conversation with him, but one which didn't find its way into the interview.

In this chapter Ezekiel has an extraordinary expressive potency. The protagonist of the passage is Jerusalem. The relationship with God and his city is described in very powerful images: 'And you grew up and became tall and arrived at full adornment. Your breasts were formed, and your hair had grown; yet you were naked and bare. When I passed by you again and saw you, behold, you were at the age for love, and I spread the corner of my garment over you and covered your nakedness; I made my vow to you and entered into a covenant with you, declares the Lord GOD, and you became mine. Then I bathed you with water and washed off your blood from you and anointed you with oil. I clothed you also with embroidered cloth and shod you with fine leather. I wrapped you in fine linen and covered you with silk. And I adorned you with ornaments and put bracelets on your wrists and a chain on your neck. And I put a ring on your nose and earrings in your ears and a beautiful crown on your head. Thus you were adorned with gold and silver, and your clothing was of fine linen and silk and embroidered cloth. You ate fine flour and honey and oil. You grew exceedingly beautiful and advanced to royalty. And your renown went forth among the nations because of your beauty, for it was perfect through the splendour that I had bestowed on you.'

And yet all this love is not enough. On the contrary: Jerusalem, infatuated by her own beauty and exploiting her fame, prostitutes herself, granting her favours to every passer-by. 'You did all these things, the deeds of a brazen prostitute, building your vaulted chamber at the head of every street, and making your lofty place in every square. Yet you were not like a prostitute, because you scorned payment. Adulterous wife, who receives strangers instead of her husband! Men give gifts to all prostitutes, but you gave your gifts to all your lovers, bribing them to come to you from every side with your whorings. So you were different from other women in your whorings. No one solicited you to play the whore, and you gave payment, while no payment was given to you; therefore you were different.' But the Lord's amorous passion overcomes everything, overcomes the feeling of hatred, of contempt, of revenge: 'But I remember the covenant I made with you when you were young, and so I will make you a promise that will last forever. When you think about how you acted, you will be ashamed, especially when I return your sisters to you as daughters, even though this was not part of our agreement. I will keep this solemn promise, and you will know that I am the LORD. I will forgive you, but you will think about your sins and be too ashamed to say a word.'

Bergoglio's prayer is not afraid of passions, or of the plastic force of the images of Ezekiel in whose pages there is not an exclusively mental vision of the relationship between God and His people, but a representation of bodies, of prostitution, of eroticism, of abandonment, of the delirium of separation, of rage, of paternal protection.

We must 'pray with the flesh, not with ideas', Pope Francis said on 5 June 2013 in his morning homily at Santa Marta. When Bergoglio speaks of the blessings he has received, he is not referring solely to a serene, idyllic, eirenic vision bound to the serene and beautiful things of life. God's blessing par excellence is his mercy, which sometimes assumes very physical images, in spite of our great sin of idolatrous prostitution that should distance us from him, but fails to do so.

With this reference to Jerusalem as an adulteress and prostitute, Pope Francis returns to the first question I asked him about his identity, to which he replied: 'I am a sinner upon whom the Lord has cast his gaze.'

This is Jorge Mario Bergoglio.

An unforgettable apricot juice

The three afternoons I spent with Pope Francis did not have a ritual setting, but felt entirely natural. I clearly remember our second encounter: I was welcomed as always by the caretaker of Santa Marta and walked to the lift. Going up with me was a nun with a white robe of the Pope's fresh from the laundry, still wrapped in transparent plastic. I said to the nun: 'It must get dirty very easily!' 'The Pope is very careful', she replied, 'and doesn't want to give us too much work.'

Reaching his floor I found the door half-open. The secretary knocked, and his voice came from inside: 'Come in, come in!' He was standing up, dealing with some papers on his desk, but immediately set them down. It was then that he said to me – I don't remember what about – 'You have to be normal. Life is normal.' And there it was; our interview was 'normal'.

It remained so even when we said goodbye after the three encounters, even though he always made sure to walk me outside and ask me insistently to pray for him. And I never gave up asking him for his blessings, which were never hasty or formal. The Pope likes laying on hands, touching the head of those he blesses, not merely tracing a gesture in the air.

Once the interview was over I needed some time to listen again to the conversation. With some passages I did that several times. I realized that it was a treasure trove. I transcribed the text and then sent it to the Pope so that he could revise it at his leisure. In fact he wanted us to revise it together, slowly rereading it in two voices: I would read one paragraph, then he would read one. I can't easily explain what it meant to run through the text and its passages out loud, point by point.

It was important to read the text out loud, because our thoughts about what to keep and what to leave out assumed the form of a lively dialogue thanks to our alternate readings. This text is the definitive integral, published one. In the present volume, in the commentary part, I have recovered a number of passages and memories because they struck me, with hindsight, as particularly significant. The Pontiff checked them personally.

As we read in turn, which obviously took a long time, eventually Pope Francis noticed that my mouth was dry. He asked me which I preferred: apricot juice or lemonade. I was struck by the unusual alternative. I chose apricot, imagining that the Pope would call someone to bring the juice.

In fact it was he who got up, took the glass, a towel and the little bottle of apricot juice and poured it for me, having a lemonade himself. I admit it: I have never particularly liked apricot juice, but from that moment it has been dear to me.

'Wake up to the World!' – Conversation with Pope Francis about the Religious Life

9.25 a.m. The New Hall of the Synod in the Vatican

When Pope Francis speaks 'off the cuff' and dialogues, his speech has a certain rhythm that 'undulates'; one would do well to follow it with care because it is fed by the relationship he experiences with his interlocutors. Those who notice should pay careful attention not only to the contents of what he says but also to the dynamic of the relationship that is created. This is what happened during the conversation that the Holy Father held with the Union of Superiors General of religious men at the end of their 82nd General Assembly.[1] Seated among them I made notes of the dialogue. I will here try to express as far as possible the richness of the contents, preserving the lively and spontaneous tone of the three-hour meeting. Halfway through the meeting, for a half-hour, the Pope circulated among the participants to greet the Superiors General personally, taking a *mate* in a relaxed and informal atmosphere.

The Superiors had, in fact, requested only a brief meeting to greet the Pope, but the Pontiff wished to spend the whole morning with them. He decided, however, neither to give a talk nor to listen to their prepared remarks: he wished to have a frank and free conversation consisting of questions and answers.

It is 9.25 and the arrival of the photographers announces the Pope's imminent entrance into the New Hall of the Synod in the Vatican, where approximately 120 Superiors await him.

Religious: sinners and prophets

Greeted by applause, the Holy Father takes a seat at exactly 9.30, looks at the clock and congratulates himself for his 'Swiss' punctuality. All laugh: the Pope wanted to greet Fr. Mauro Jöhri this way: he is Swiss and the Minister General of the Capuchin Friars Minor who had just been elected vice-president of the Union of Superiors General.

After a few brief words of greeting from the president, Fr. Adolfo Nicolás, the Superior General of the Jesuits, and from the general secretary, Fr. David Glenday, a Comboni Missionary, Pope Francis cordially thanked the Assembly in a very simple way for its invitation; the first group of questions began immediately thereafter. The religious questioned the

Pope especially about the identity and the mission of religious: 'What do you expect of consecrated life? What do you ask of us? If you were in our place what would you do to respond to your call to go to the frontiers, to live the Gospel *sine glossa*, evangelical prophecy? What should we hear you calling us to do?' And further: 'What should be emphasized today? What are the priorities?'

Pope Francis began by saying that he, too, is a religious, and he therefore knows from experience what they were talking about.[2] The last Pope who belonged to a religious order was the Camaldolese Gregory XVI, elected in 1831. He then made explicit reference to Benedict XVI: 'He said that the Church grows through witness, not by proselytism. The witness that can really attract is that associated with attitudes which are uncommon: generosity, detachment, sacrifice, self-forgetfulness in order to care for others. This is the witness, the "martyrdom" of religious life. It "sounds an alarm" for people. Religious say to people with their life: "What's happening?" These people are telling me something! These people go beyond a mundane horizon. Thus,' continued the Pope, quoting Benedict XVI, 'religious life ought to promote growth in the Church by way of attraction.[3]

'The Church', therefore, 'must be attractive. Wake up the world! Be witnesses of a different way of doing things, of acting, of living! It is possible to live differently in this world. We are speaking of an eschatological outlook, of the values of the Kingdom incarnated here, on this earth. It is a question of leaving everything to follow the Lord. No, I do not want to say "radical". Evangelical radicalness is not only for religious: it is demanded of all. But religious follow the Lord in a special way, in a prophetic way. It is this witness that I expect of you. Religious should be men and women who are able to wake the world up.'

Pope Francis has returned in a circular fashion to concepts that he has already touched on, exploring them more deeply. In fact he continued: 'You should be real witnesses of a way of doing and acting differently. But in life it is difficult for everything to be clear, precise, outlined neatly. Life is complicated; it consists of grace and sin. He who does not sin is not human. We all make mistakes and we need to recognize our weakness. A religious who recognizes himself as weak and a sinner does not negate the witness that he is called to give, rather he reinforces it, and this is good for everyone. What I expect of you therefore is to give witness. I want this special witness from religious.'

'Avoid fundamentalism and light the way to the future'

Continuing his response to the first questions, Pope Francis touched on one of the key points of his thinking: 'I am convinced of one thing: the great changes in history were realized when reality was seen not from the centre but rather from the periphery. It is a hermeneutical question: reality is understood only if it is looked at from the periphery, and not when our viewpoint is equidistant from everything. Truly to understand reality we need to move away from the central position of calmness and peacefulness and direct ourselves to the peripheral areas.[4] Being at the periphery helps to see and to understand better, to analyze reality more correctly, to shun centralism and approaches based on ideology.'

Therefore, 'It is not a good strategy to be at the centre of a sphere. To understand we ought to move around, to see reality from various viewpoints.[5] We ought to get used to thinking. I often refer to a letter of Father Pedro Arrupe, who had been General of the Society of Jesus. It was a letter directed to the *Centros de Investigación y Acción Social* (CIAS). In this letter Father Arrupe spoke of poverty and said that some time of real contact with the poor is necessary. This is really very important to me: the need to become acquainted with reality by experience, to spend time walking on the periphery in order really to become acquainted with the reality and life experiences of people. If this does not happen we then run the risk of being abstract ideologists or fundamentalists, which is not healthy.'[6]

The Pope lingered on a concrete issue, that of the apostolate to youth. 'Those who work with youth cannot be content with simply saying things that are too tidy and structured, as in a tract; these things go in one ear and out the other of young people. We need a new language, a new way of saying things. Today God asks this of us: to leave the nest which encloses us in order to be sent. He who lives his consecration in a cloister lives this interior tension in prayer so that the Gospel might grow. The fulfilment of the evangelical command "Go to the whole world and proclaim the Gospel to every creature" (Mk 16.15) can be accomplished with this hermeneutical key shifted to the existential and geographical periphery. It is the most concrete way of imitating Jesus, who went toward all the peripheries. Jesus went to all, really all. I would not really feel uncomfortable going to the periphery: you should not feel uncomfortable in reaching out to anyone.'

What, therefore, is the priority of consecrated life? The Pope answered: 'Prophecy of the Kingdom, which is a non-negotiable. The emphasis should fall on being prophets, and not in playing at being them. Naturally the devil hurls his temptations at us; one of them is: just appear to be prophets. But it is not possible simply to play at these things. I myself have seen very sad things in this regard. No: religious are men and women who light the way to the future.'

In his interview with *La Civiltà Cattolica* Pope Francis had clearly stated that religious are called to a prophetic life. This is what is particular to them: 'to be prophets, in particular, by demonstrating how Jesus lived on this earth, and to proclaim how the Kingdom of God will be in its perfection. A religious must never give up prophesizing. [...] Let us think about what so many great saints, monks and religious men and women have done, from St Anthony the Abbot onward. Being prophets may sometimes involve making *ruido* [Spanish for noise]. I do not know how to put it... Prophecy makes noise, uproar, some say "a mess". But in reality, the charism of religious people is like yeast: prophecy announces the spirit of the Gospel.'

So, how to be prophets living one's own particular religious charism? For Pope Francis there is a need 'to reinforce that which is institutional in consecrated life and not confuse the Religious Institute with apostolic work. The former lasts; the latter fades away.' The Pope continues: 'The charism lasts, is strong; the work fades away. Sometimes the Religious Institute and the work are confused. The Institute is creative, is always looking for outlets. In this way too the peripheries change and a checklist can be made that is always different.'

'The charism is not a bottle of distilled water'

At this point the questions asked centred around themes of vocations. We are witnessing a profound change in the human geography of the Church and so too of religious orders. Vocations in Africa and Asia are increasing, which alone accounts for most of their total number. All this poses a series of challenges: inculturation of the charism, vocational discernment and the selection of candidates, the challenge of inter-religious dialogue, the search for a more equitable representation in the governmental organizations of the orders and, more generally, in the structure of the Church. The Pope was thus asked to offer some guidance concerning this.

Pope Francis says that he is well aware of the many geographical changes in consecrated life and that 'all cultures are able to be called by the Lord, that he is free to stir up more vocations in one part of the world than in another. What does the Lord wish to say by sending us vocations from the youngest Churches? I don't know. But I ask myself the question. We have to ask it. The Lord's will is somehow in all this.

'There are Churches who are bearing new fruit. At one time they perhaps were not so fertile, but they are now. This necessitates, of course, rethinking the inculturation of the charism. The charism is one but, as St Ignatius used to say, it needs to be lived according to the places, times and persons.

'The charism is not a bottle of distilled water. It needs to be lived energetically as well as reinterpreted culturally. But in this way there is the danger of making a mistake, of committing errors. It is risky. Certainly, certainly: we will always make mistakes, no doubt about it. But this should not stop us, because there is the chance of making worse mistakes. In fact we should always ask for forgiveness and look shamefully upon apostolic failures due to a lack of courage. Just think, for example, of the brilliant intuitions of Matteo Ricci which were simply allowed to evaporate.[8]

'I am not referring to folkloric adaptations of customs,' the Pope continued, 'it is a question of mentality, of a mindset. For example, there are peoples who think in a more concrete than abstract way, or at least in a kind of abstraction different from that in the West. I lived this difference myself when I was the Jesuit Provincial in Argentina. I remember how much effort a Jesuit Brother and I expended when we talked even about simple things of daily life; he was from an area where the Guarini live, a people who have developed a very concrete way of thinking.

'We need to live courageously and face these challenges when they deal with important subjects as well. In the end a person cannot be formed as religious without taking his or her life, experience, mentality and cultural context into account. This is the way to proceed. This is what the great religious missionaries did. The extraordinary adventures of the Spanish Jesuit Segundo Llorente come to mind, a tenacious and contemplative missionary in Alaska. He not only learned the language but also the concrete way of thinking of the people.[9]

'Inculturating the charism, therefore, is fundamental, and this never means relativizing it. We must not make the charism rigid or uniform. When we make our cultures uniform we kill the charism', the Pontiff concluded decisively, indicating the necessity of 'introducing persons of various cultures into the central governance of the Orders and Congregations, who express diverse ways of living the charism.'

Pope Francis is certainly aware of the risks, even in terms of 'vocational recruitment' by younger Churches. He recalled, inter alia, that in 1994, in the context of the Ordinary Synod on Consecrated Life and the Missions, the Filipino bishops criticized the 'novice trade', that is, massive arrival of foreign congregations who were opening houses in the archipelago with an eye toward recruiting vocations to be transplanted to Europe. 'We need to keep our eyes open for such situations', the Pope said.

He also spent some time on the vocation of brothers and, more generally, religious who are not priests. He complained that an adequate awareness of this specific vocation has not yet been developed. He referred to a document related to this which has never appeared, and which might be revisited.

At this point the Pope signalled to Cardinal João Braz de Aviz, Prefect of the Congregation of Institutes of Consecrated Life and Societies of Apostolic Life, and to the secretary of that Congregation, Monsignor José Rodríguez Carballo, who were present in the Assembly, inviting them to consider the question. He concluded: 'I do not actually believe that the vocational crisis among religious who are not priests is a sign of the times telling us that this vocation has ended. We should rather understand what God is asking us.' Answering a question concerning religious brothers as superiors in clerical orders, the Pope replied that this was a canonical issue that needs to be dealt with at that level.

'Formation is a work of art, not a police action'

Pope Francis then listened to a few questions about formation. He answered immediately, indicating his priorities: 'The formation of candidates is fundamental. There are four pillars of formation: spiritual, intellectual, communitarian and apostolic. The evil to fight against is the image of religious life understood as an escape or hiding place in face of an "external", difficult and complex world. The four pillars should be integrated right from the first day of entrance into the noviceship, and should not be arranged sequentially. They must be interactive.'

The Pope is aware of the fact that the problem of formation today is not easy to deal with: 'Daily culture is much richer and conflictual than that which we experienced in our day, years ago. Our culture was simpler and more ordered. Inculturation today calls for a different attitude. For example: problems are not solved simply by forbidding doing this or that. Dialogue as well as confrontation are needed. To avoid problems, in some houses of formation, young people grit their teeth, try not to make mistakes, follow the rules smiling a lot, just waiting for the day when they are told: "Good. You have finished formation." This is hypocrisy that is the result of clericalism, which is one of the worst evils. I said as much to the bishops of the Latin American Bishops Council (CELAM) this summer in Rio de Janeiro: we need to conquer this propensity toward clericalism in houses of formation and seminaries too. I summarize by some advice that I once received as a young man: "If you want to advance, think clearly and speak obscurely." That was a clear invitation to hypocrisy. We need to avoid that at all costs.' As a matter of fact, in Rio the Pope identified clericalism as one of the causes of the 'lack of maturity and Christian freedom' in the People of God.[10]

It follows that 'If the seminary is too large, it ought to be divided into smaller communities with directors who are equipped really to accompany those in their charge. Dialogue must be serious, without fear, sincere. It is important to recall that the language of young people in formation today is different from that in the past: we are living through an epochal change. Formation is a work of art, not a police action. We must form their hearts. Otherwise we are creating little monsters. And then these little monsters mould the People of God. This really gives me goose pimples.'

The Pope then insisted on the fact that formation should not be oriented only toward personal growth but also in view of its final goal: the People of God. It is important to think about the people to whom these persons will be sent while forming them: 'We must always think of the faithful, of the faithful

People of God. Persons must be formed who are witnesses of the resurrection of Jesus. The director should keep in mind that the person in formation will be called to care for the People of God. We always must think of the People of God in all of this. Just think of religious who have hearts that are as sour as vinegar: they are not made for the people. In the end we must not form administrators, managers, but fathers, brothers, travelling companions.'

Finally, Pope Francis wanted to highlight a further risk: 'accepting a young man in a seminary who has been asked to leave a religious order because of problems with formation and for serious reasons is a huge problem. I am not speaking about people who recognize that they are sinners: we are all sinners, but we are not all corrupt. Sinners are accepted, but not people who are corrupt.' Here the Pope recalled Benedict XVI's important decision in dealing with cases of abuse: 'this should be a lesson to us to have the courage to approach personal formation as a serious challenge, always keeping in mind the People of God.'

Living brotherhood by 'soothing conflicts'

The Synod on the New Evangelization had asked religious to be witnesses to the humanizing power of the Gospel through a life of brotherhood. Taking a cue from this call, the Pope was asked a few questions about how religious should live together as brothers: 'How can we keep commitments of the mission as well as those of community life? How can we combat the tendency toward individualism? How should we act toward brothers in difficulty or who live or create conflict? How can we combine justice and mercy in difficult cases?'

Pope Francis recounted that the previous day he met with the prior of Taizé, Frère Alois: 'There are Catholic, Calvinist, Lutheran, etc. monks at Taizé… They all live a real life of brotherhood together. They are an impressive apostolic role model for young people. The fraternal community has an enormous power to call people together. The malaise of the community, on the other hand, has power that destroys. The temptation against fraternity is that which is the most disruptive to progress in consecrated life. St John Berchmans[11] used to say that his greatest penance was precisely community life. Sometimes living fraternally is difficult, but if it is not lived it is not productive. Work, even that which is "apostolic", can become an escape from fraternal life. If a person cannot live brotherhood he cannot live religious life.

'Religious brotherhood,' continued the Pope, 'with all its possible diversity, is an experience of love that goes beyond conflicts. Community conflicts are inevitable: in a certain sense they need to happen, if the community is truly living sincere and honest relationships. That's life. It does not make sense to think of living in a community in which there are brothers who are not experiencing difficulties in their lives. Something is missing from communities where there is no conflict. Reality dictates that there are conflicts in all families and all groups of people. And conflict must be faced head on: it should not be ignored. Covering it over just creates a pressure cooker that will eventually explode. A life without conflicts is not life.'

The stakes at play are high. We know that one of the fundamental principles of Pope Francis is that 'unity is superior to conflict'. His words to religious should be read in light of *Evangelii gaudium* (n. 226–30), where he wonders about 'the acceptance of bearing conflict, of resolving it and transforming it into a link that leads to a new process' (n. 227). It is important to recall that for Bergoglio personal fulfilment is never an exclusively individual under-taking, but collective, communitarian.[12] Conflict in this sense can, and even should, evolve in a process of maturation.

In any case conflict must be approached with spiritual counselling: 'We should never act like the priest or levite in the parable of the good Samaritan, who just walked by. But what should we do? I recall', says the Pope, 'the story of a young man, 22 years old, who was suffering from a deep depression. I am not speaking of a religious, but of a young man who lived with his mother, who was a widow and who did the laundry of wealthy families. This young man no longer went to work and lived in an alcoholic haze. The mother was not able to help him: every morning before leaving she would simply look at him with great tenderness. Today this young man has a position of responsibility: he overcame that problem, because in the end that look of tenderness from his mother shook him up. We have to recapture that tenderness, including maternal tenderness. Think of the tenderness that St Francis lived, for example. Tenderness helps to overcome conflicts. If this is insufficient, it might be necessary to change communities.

'It is true,' Pope Francis continued, 'sometimes we are very cruel. We all experience the temptation to criticize for personal satisfaction or to gain personal advantage. Sometimes the problems in the brotherhood are due to fragile personalities, in which case the help of a professional, a psychologist, should be sought. There is no need to be afraid of this: one need not fear necessarily succumbing to psycho-babble. But never, never should we act like managers when dealing with conflicts in the brotherhood. We should involve the heart.

'Brotherhood is a delicate thing. In the hymn of First Vespers of the Solemnity of St Joseph in the Argentine breviary, the Saint is asked to take care of the Church with *ternura de eucaristía*, "Eucharistic tenderness".[13] This is how we should treat brothers: with Eucharistic tenderness. We need to caress conflicts. I recall when Paul VI received a child's letter with many drawings. Paul said that the reception of such a letter on a desk covered only with letters that dealt with problems did him a lot of good. Tenderness does us good. Eucharistic tenderness does not mask conflict but rather helps us to confront it like people.'

The mutual relations between religious and local Churches

At this point the Superiors General asked the Pope several questions regarding the activities of religious communities in the context of local Churches and about their relationship with bishops: how can the charisms of the various orders be both respected and promoted for the welfare of the Church where they live and work? How can communion among the distinct charisms and forms of Christian life be fostered so as to cultivate the growth of all and a better development of mission?

Pope Francis answered that the request to review the directive criteria that were promulgated in 1978 by the Congregation for Religious and by the Congregation for Bishops (*Mutuae relationes*) concerning the relations between bishops and religious in the Church has been pending for quite a few years now. The Pope is of the opinion that the time is ripe now because 'that document was useful at the time but is now outdated. The charisms of the various religious orders need to be respected and fostered because they are needed in dioceses. I know the problems through personal experience', he continued, 'the problems that can arise between a bishop and religious communities.' For example, 'if the religious decide one day to withdraw from one of their works due to a lack of manpower, the bishop often finds himself suddenly left with a hot potato in his hand. I myself have had such difficult experiences. I would be informed that a work was being dropped and I did not know what to do. I was once actually told after the event. On the other hand I can also speak about other, positive developments. The fact is: I know the problems, but I also know that the bishops are not always acquainted with the charisms and works of religious. We bishops need to understand that consecrated persons are not functionaries but gifts that enrich dioceses. The involvement of religious communities in dioceses is important. Dialogue between the bishop and religious must be rescued so that, due to a lack of understanding of their charisms, bishops do not view religious simply as useful instruments.' It was for this reason that the Pope entrusted to the Congregation for Religious the task of studying the document *Mutuae relationes* and to work on a revision.

The frontiers of mission: Marginalization, culture and education

The last questions once again brought up the frontiers of the mission of consecrated persons. The Pope has often spoken about 'departing', 'going' and 'frontiers'. The Superiors General, therefore, inquired what these frontiers might be for which we should embark: 'How do you see the presence of consecrated life in the context of "exclusion" in our world of marginalization? Many orders are engaged in the work of education: how do you see this kind of service? What would you say to religious who are engaged in this field?'

First of all, the Pope states that geographical frontiers certainly remain, and that it is necessary to be ready to move. But there are also symbolic frontiers that are not predetermined and are not the same for everyone; rather they 'need to be sought on the basis of the charisms of each Order. Discernment, therefore, should be undertaken in this context of one's own charism. The realities of exclusion certainly remain the most significant priorities, but they call for discernment.

The first criterion is to send the best, most gifted people into these situations of exclusion and marginalization. These are the most risky situations and call for courage and a great deal of prayer. And it is necessary that superiors support and encourage the people dedicated to this work.' There is always the risk, the Pope recalled, of being overcome by enthusiasm; this might result in sending religious who have good will but who are not prepared for situations they will find at the frontiers of the marginalized where they are sent. We must not make decisions concerning the marginalized without being sure of adequate discernment and support.

Besides this challenge of the marginalized, the Pope referred to two other ever-present and important challenges: one cultural and the other having to do with education in schools and universities. Consecrated life can be of great service in these areas. He recalled: 'When the Fathers of *La Civiltà Cattolica* came to visit me I spoke with them about the frontiers of thought, thought that is unique and weak. I recommended this frontier to them. As the major rector of the Salesians knows, everything for them began on the basis of a dream of education at the frontier, the dream of Don Bosco that thrust his Salesians to the geographical peripheries of Patagonia. We could give many other examples.'

The pillars of education, according to the Pope, are: 'convey understanding, convey ways of doing things, convey values. Faith is conveyed through these. The educator should be up to being a person who educates, he or she should consider how to proclaim

Jesus Christ to a generation that is changing.' He insisted therefore: 'Education today is a key, key, key mission!' And he recalled some of his experiences in Buenos Aires regarding the preparation necessary to welcome children in an educational context, little boys and girls, young adults who live in complex situations, especially family ones: 'I remember the case of a very sad little girl who finally confided to her teacher the reason for her state of mind: "My mother's fiancé doesn't like me."

'The percentage of children studying in schools who have separated parents is very high. The situation in which we live now provides us with new challenges which sometimes are difficult for us to understand. How can we proclaim Christ to these boys and girls? How can we proclaim Christ to a generation that is changing? We must be careful not to administer to them a vaccine against faith.'[14]

**

At the end of three hours, around 12.30, the Pope said he was sorry to have to end the conversation: 'Let's leave some questions for next time', he said, smiling. He confessed that the dentist was waiting for him. Before saying goodbye to the Superiors General he had an announcement to make: 2015 will be a year dedicated to consecrated life; these words were greeted with a long applause. The Pontiff looked smiling at the Prefect and the Secretary for the Congregation for Religious and of Institutes of Apostolic Life, saying 'it's their fault; it's one of their ideas: it's dangerous when these two get together', provoking laughter among all in the Assembly.

As he left the hall he stated: 'I thank you, I thank you for this act of faith that you have made in this meeting. Thank you for what you do, for your spirit of faith and your pursuit of service. Thank you for your witness, for the martyrs that you continue to give to the Church, as well for the humiliations to which you must submit: this is the way of the Cross. Thank you from the bottom of my heart.'

Speech by Pope Francis to the community of the writer of La Civiltà Cattolica

Sala dei Papi
Friday 14 June 2013

Dear Friends in the Lord,

I am happy to meet with you, writers, your whole community, the Sisters and the staff of the administration of the House. Since 1850, the Jesuits of *La Civiltà Cattolica* have been engaged in a work that has a particular link with the Pope and the Apostolic See. My predecessors, meeting with you in audience, acknowledged many times how this link is an essential feature of your review. Today I would like to suggest three words to you that might help you in your endeavour.

The first is dialogue. You carry out an important cultural service. Initially the attitude and *La Civiltà Cattolica* was combative and often, also, harshly combative, in tune with the general atmosphere of the time. Reviewing the 163 years of the review, one gathers a rich variety of positions, due be it to the changing of the historical circumstances, be it to the personality of the individual writers. Your fidelity to the Church still requires that you be hard against hypocrisies, fruit of a closed, sick heart, hard against this sickness. However, your main task is not to build walls but bridges; it is to establish a dialogue with all men, also with those who do not share the Christian faith, but 'have the veneration of high human values', and even 'with those who oppose the Church and persecute her in various ways' (*Gaudium et spes*, 92).

There are so many human questions to discuss and share and it is always possible to approach the truth in dialogue, which is a gift of God, and to enrich ourselves mutually. To dialogue means to be convinced that the other has something good to say, to make room for his point of view, for his opinion, for his proposals without falling, obviously, into relativism. And to dialogue it is necessary to lower one's defences and to open the doors. Continue your dialogue with the cultural, social and political institutions, also to offer your contribution to the formation of citizens who have the good of all at heart and work for the common good. The '*civiltà cattolica*' is the civilization of love, of mercy and of faith.

The second word is discernment. Your task is to gather and express the expectations, the desires, the joys and the dramas of our time, and to offer the elements for a reading of the reality in the light of the Gospel. The great spiritual questions are more alive today than ever, but there is need of someone to interpret them

168

and to understand them. With humble and open intelligence, 'seek and find God in all things', as St Ignatius wrote. God is at work in the life of every man and in the culture: the Spirit blows where it will. Seek to discover what God has operated and how His work will proceed. A treasure of the Jesuits is in fact spiritual discernment, which seeks to recognize the presence of the Spirit of God in the human and cultural reality, the seed of His presence already planted in the events, in the sensibilities, in the desires, in the profound tensions of hearts and of the social, cultural and spiritual contexts. I recall something that Rahner said: the Jesuit is a specialist of discernment in the field of God and also in the field of the devil. One must not be afraid to continue in discernment to find the truth. When I read these observations of Rahner, they really struck me.

And to seek God in all things, in all fields of knowledge, of art, of science, of political, social and economic life, studies, sensibility and experience are necessary. Some of the subjects you address might not have an explicit relation with a Christian perspective, but they are important to appreciate the way that persons understand themselves and the world that surrounds them. Your informative observation must be broad, objective and timely. It is also necessary to give particular attention into the truth, goodness and beauty of God, which are always considered together, and are precious allies in the commitment to defend the dignity of man, in the building of peaceful coexistence and in protecting creation carefully. From this attention stems serene, sincere and strong judgement about events, illuminated by Christ. Great figures such as Matteo Ricci are a model of this. All this requires keeping the heart and mind open, avoiding the spiritual sickness of self-reference. Even the Church, when she becomes self-referencing, gets sick, grows old. May our sight, well fixed on Christ, be prophetic and dynamic towards the future: in this way, you will always be young and audacious in the reading of events!

The third word is frontier. The mission of a review of culture such as *La Civiltà Cattolica* enters the contemporary cultural debate and proposes, in a serious and at the same time accessible way, the vision that comes from the Christian faith. The break between Gospel and culture is undoubtedly a tragedy (cf. *Evangelii nuntiandi*, 20). You are called to give your contribution to heal this break, which passes also through the heart of each one of you and of your readers. This ministry is typical of the mission of the Society of Jesus. With your reflections and your deeper analyses, support the cultural and social processes, and all those going through difficult transitions, taking account also of the conflicts. Your proper place is the frontiers. This is the place of Jesuits. That which Paul VI, taken up by Benedict

XVI, said of the Society of Jesus is particularly true for you today: 'Wherever in the Church, even in the most difficult and acute fields, in the crossroads of ideologies, in the social trenches, there was and is the confrontation between the burning exigencies of man and the perennial message of the Gospel, the Jesuits have been and are there.'

Please, be men of the frontier, with that capacity that comes from God (cf. 2 Cor. 3.6). But do not fall into the temptation of taming the frontiers: you must go to the frontiers and not bring the frontiers home to varnish them a bit and tame them. In today's world, subject to rapid changes and agitated by questions of great relevance for the life of the faith, a courageous commitment is urgent to educate to a faith of conviction and maturity, capable of giving meaning to life and of offering convincing answers to all those seeking God. It is a question of supporting the action of the Church in all fields of her mission. This year *La Civiltà Cattolica* has been renewed: it has assumed a new graphic appearance, it can also be read in a digital version and it brings its readers together also in the social networks. These are also frontiers in which you are called to operate. Continue on this path!

Dear Fathers, I see young, less young and elderly among you. Yours is a unique review of its kind, which is born from a community of life and of studies;

as in a harmonious choir, each one must have his voice and harmonize it with that of others. Strength, dear brothers! I am sure I can count on you. While I entrust you to the *Madonna della Strada*, I impart to you, writers, collaborators and Sisters, as well as to all readers of the review, my Blessing.

NOTES

Santa Marta, Monday, 19 August, 9.50 a.m.

1   J. M. Bergoglio, *Noi come cittadini. Noi come popolo. Verso un bicentenario in giustizia e solidarietà 2010–2016*, Jaca Book – Libreria Editrice Vaticana, Milan – Vatican City 2013, p. 68.

2   Cf. J. M. Bergoglio, *Aprite la mente al vostro cuore*, Rizzoli, Milano 2013, p. 41.

3   J. M. Bergoglio, *È l'amore che apre gli occhi*, Rizzoli, Milan 2013.

4   A. J. Heschel, *Il messaggio dei profeti*, Borla, Rome 1981, p. 116.

5   Homily of Holy Father Francis, St Peter's Square, Sunday, 13 October 2013. All of the specches and homilies of Holy Father Francis can be consulted on the website of the Holy See, www.vatican.va.

Chapter I

1   J. M. Bergoglio, Papa Francesco. *Il nuovo Papa si racconta, conversazione con F. Ambrogetti e S. Rubin*, Salani, Milan 2013, pp. 41–2.

2   Quoted in: S. Falasca, *La «confessione» di padre Bergoglio*, 'Avvenire', 31 March 2013.

3   J. M. Bergoglio, *Dio nella città*, São Paulo, Cinisello Balsamo (MI) 2013, p. 32.

4   J. M. Bergoglio, *Scegliere la vita. Proposte per tempi difficili*, Bompiani, Milan 2013, p. 78.

5   J. M. Bergoglio, *Meditaciones para religiosos*, Diego de Torres, San Miguel 1982.

6   J. M. Bergoglio, *Scegliere la vita*, p. 70.

7   Ibid., p. 71.

8   Ibid., p. 72.

9   J. M. Bergoglio, *Disciplina e passione. Le sfide di oggi per chi deve educare*, Bompiani, Milan 2013, p. 45.

10   J. M. Bergoglio, Papa Francesco. *Il nuovo Papa si racconta*, p. 45

11   Cf. N. Scavo, *La lista di Bergoglio. I salvati da Francesco durante la dittatura. La storia mai raccontata*, Emi, Bologna 2013.

Chapter II

1   Speech by His Holiness Pope Francis during the meeting with the Brazilian Bishops, Saturday, 27 July 2013.

2   Press conference by Holy Father Francis on his flight back from Rio de Janeiro, Sunday, 28 July 2013.

3   The video of the interview can be seen at g1.globo.com. The text was translated into Italian by the *Osservatore Romano* and can be read on the newspaper's website, www.osservatoreromano.va.

4   Cf. J. M. Bergoglio, *In Lui solo la speranza.*

Esercizi spirituali ai vescovi spagnoli (15–22 gennaio 2006), Jaca Book – Libreria Editrice Vaticana, Milan – Vatican City 2013, p. 56.

5 Address by Pope Francis during his visit to the community of Varginha (Manguinhos), Rio de Janeiro, Thursday, 25 July 2013.

6 Address by Pope Francis during his visit to the Ospedale de São Francisco de Assis na Providência, Rio de Janeiro, Wedenesday, 24 July 2013.

7 J. M. Bergoglio, *Nel cuore dell'uomo. Utopia e impegno*, Bompiani, Milan 2013, p. 54.

8 A. Tornielli, *Francesco insieme*, Piemme, Milan 2013, p. 86.

9 J. M. Bergoglio, *Scegliere la vita*, p. 78.

10 Ibid., p. 80.

11 Ibid., p. 76.

12 J. M. Bergoglio, Papa Francesco. *Il nuovo Papa si racconta*, p. 85.

13 Ibid., p. 87.

14 J. M. Bergoglio, *Scegliere la vita*, p. 76.

15 J. M. Bergoglio, *Varcare la soglia della fede. Lettera all'Arcidiocesi di Buenos Aires per l'Anno della Fede*, Libreria Editrice Vaticana, Vatican City 2013, p. 25.

16 Ibid., p. 51.

17 A. Tornielli, *Francesco insieme*.

18 Homily on the occasion of the prayer in memory of witnesses of the faith at the Church of Our

Lady of Carmen in Buenos Aires, 10 April 2001.

19 Homily by the Holy Father during Holy Mass with the bishops of the XXVIII World Youth Day and with the priests, religious and seminarians, Cathedral of San Sebastian, Rio de Janeiro, Saturday, 27 July 2013.

20 J. M. Bergoglio, *Nel cuore dell'uomo*, p. 23.

21 Address of Pope Francis during his meeting with the Bishops of Brazil, Archbishop's House, Rio de Janeiro, Saturday, 27 July 2013.

22 Ibid.

23 Address of Pope Francis during his audience with all the Cardinals, Sala Clementina, Friday, 15 March 2013.

24 J. M. Bergoglio, *Nel cuore dell'uomo*, p. 15.

25 J. M. Bergoglio, *Noi come cittadini. Noi come popolo*, p. 69.

26 J. M. Bergoglio, *Nel cuore dell'uomo*, p. 8.

27 J. M. Bergoglio, *Scegliere la vita*, p. 14.

28 Y. Congar, *Vera e falsa riforma nella Chiesa*, Jaca Book, Milan 1994, p. 155.

Chapter III

1 J. M. Bergoglio, *Scegliere la vita*, p. 9.

2 Cf. J. M. Bergoglio, *Dio nella città*, p. 31.

3 J. M. Bergoglio, *È l'amore che apre gli occhi*, p. 146.

4 Cf. J. M. Bergoglio, *Disciplina e passione*, p. 42.

5   J. M. Bergoglio, *Noi come cittadini. Noi come popolo*, p. 26.

6   J. M. Bergoglio, *Nel cuore dell'uomo*, cit., p. 7.

7   Discorso del Santo Padre Francesco in occasione dell'incontro con i vescovi responsabili del Consiglio Episcopale Latinoamericano (CELAM), Centro Studi di Sumaré, Rio de Janeiro, Sunday, 28 July 2013.

8   J. M. Bergoglio, *Nel cuore dell'uomo*, p. 8.

9   J. M. Bergoglio, *Scegliere la vita*, p. 28.

10 *Quello che avrei detto al concistoro, intervista di S. Falasca al cardinale J. M. Bergoglio*, «30Giorni», November 2007.

11 J. M. Bergoglio, *Varcare la soglia della fede*, p. 33.

12 J. M. Bergoglio, *Scegliere la vita*, p. 8.

13 Prefazione a G. Tantardini, *Il tempo della Chiesa secondo Agostino*, Città Nuova, Rome 2009. Anche in www.30giorni.it/articoli_id_21809_l1.htm.

14 J. M. Bergoglio, A. Skorka, *On Heaven and Earth*, Bloomsbury, London, 2013, p. 13 ff.

15 Ibid., p. 24.

16 J. M. Bergoglio, *Scegliere la vita*, p. 8.

Chapter IV

1   J. M. Bergoglio, *Scegliere la vita*, p. 64.

2   J. M. Bergoglio, *Noi come cittadini. Noi come popolo*, p. 40 ff.

3   Ibid., pp. 37–9.

4   Cf. J. M. Bergoglio, *Religiosidad popular como inculturación de la fe*, 19 January 2008.

5   The text has been translated into Italian, with the title *Bergoglio, Borges e qualche sorpresa*, by the website Terre d'America (www.terredamerica. com) 16 May 2013.

6   J. M. Bergoglio, Papa Francesco. *Il nuovo Papa si racconta*, p. 157.

Chapter V

1   J. M. Bergoglio, *Solo l'amore ci può salvare*, Libreria Editrice Vaticana, Vatican City 2013, p. 134.

2   J. M. Bergoglio, Papa Francesco. *Il nuovo Papa si racconta*, p. 48.

3   J. M. Bergoglio, *Disciplina e passione*, p. 31 ff.

4   J. M. Bergoglio, *Papa Francesco. Il nuovo Papa si racconta*, p. 121.

Chapter VI

1   The Assembly took place from November 27 to 29 at the *Salesianum* in Rome. It consisted of a meeting based on three experiences that guided the reflections that followed. Fr. Janson Hervé of the Little Brothers of Jesus spoke of the 'lights that help me to live this service to my brothers and how Pope Francis encourages my hope'. Fr. Mauro Jöhri, a Capuchin, explained 'how Pope Francis is inspiring me and challenging me in the service of directing my Order'. Finally, Fr. Hainz Kulüke of the Society of the Divine Word dwelt on 'leadership inside a missionary religious Congregation in an international and intercultural context in light of the example of Pope Francis."

2   Recall that J. M. Bergoglio as provincial of the Jesuits in Argentina had published *Meditaciones para religiosos*, San Miguel: Ediciones Dieo de Torres, 1982, a book consisting of a collection of a series of reflections given to his confreres. They are useful in shedding light on several key themes that Bergoglio will develop later.

3   Benedict XVI, Homily at the inaugural Mass of the General Episcopal Conference of Latin America and the Caribbean at the Shrine of Aparecida (13 May 2007). Pope Francis has taken up this theme of his predecessor a

number of times. He did so in his homily at Santa Marta on 1 October, adding: 'When people see this witness of humility, of meekness, of gentleness, they hear the need of which the prophet Zachariah speaks: "I wish to come with you!" People sense this need when faced with the witness of charity, that humble charity without pretence, not self-important, humble, which adores and serves.' The quotation from Benedict XVI is repeated in Pope Francis' speech of 4 October during his visit to the cathedral of San Rufino in Assisi, as well as in the Apostolic Exhortation *Evangelii gaudium* (n. 14).

4   Cf. J. M. Bergoglio, *Nel cuore dell'uomo. Utopia e impegno*, Milan: Bompiani, 2013, p. 23; Pope Francis, *La mia porta è sempre aperta. Une conversazione con Antonio Spadaro*, Milan: Rizzoli, 2013, p. 86ff.

5   Pope Francis has expressed this conviction in *Evangelii guadium* where he wrote: 'Here our model is not the sphere, which is no greater than its parts, where every point is equidistant from the centre, and there are no differences between them. Instead, it is the polyhedron, which reflects the convergence of all its parts, each of which preserves its distinc tiveness." (236)

6   Pope Francis is well acquainted with this letter

of Father Pedro Arrupe and also quoted it in his interview with *La Civiltà Cattolica*, describing it as 'inspired'. Cf. Pope Francis, *La mia porta è sempre aperta...*, p. 117.

7   Ibid. p. 63f.

8   The lack of understanding was due to the fact that, in their missions, the Jesuits were trying to adapt the proclamation of the Gospel to the local culture and rituals. This worried some, and several voices were raised in the Church that objected to the spirit of such an approach, fearing that it might contaminate the Christian message. Prophetic positions are not usually accepted when formulated because they go beyond the ordinary way of understanding the facts.

9   Father Segundo Llorente (Mansilla, Mayor, León [Spain], 18 November 1906 — Spokane, Washington [USA] 26 January 1989), a Spanish Jesuit who spent more than 40 years as a missionary in Alaska. He was the Representative to the United States Congress from the State of Alaska, of which he is considered a co-founder. He was buried in an Indian cemetery in De Smet, Idaho, where only indigenous native Americans can be buried. When he arrived in Akulurak at the age of 29 his first problem consisted not only of learning Eskimo but also of speaking about God to people with a

radically different way of thinking from that of Europe. He wrote 12 books about his missionary experience.

10   Ibid. Speech during a meeting with the coordinators of the Latin American Bishops Council (CELAM) during the general organizational meeting at the Centro Studi di Sumaré, Rio de Janeiro, 28 July 2012.

11   John (Jan) Berchmans (Diest [Belgium], 12 March 1599 — Rome, 13 August 1621) was a Jesuit, canonized by Pope Leo XIII in 1888. He pronounced his first religious profession as a Jesuit on 24 September 1618 and moved to Rome to complete his philosophical studies at the Roman College, where he fell ill. He died only two years later, on 13 August 1621. True to his favourite mottos: *Age quod agis* (Do what you are doing well) and *Maximi facere minima* (Do the most with the least), he succeeded in accomplishing ordinary things in an extraordinary way and became the patron saint of community life.

12   Cf. J. M. Bergoglio, *È l'amore che apre gli occhi*, Milan: Rizzoli, 2013, p. 46.

13   *Guarda a la Iglesia de quien fue figura / la inmaculada y maternal María; / guárdala intacta, firme y con ternura / de eucaristía.*

14   Pope Francis has lingered here for a while in the past, on themes about education in various

interventions in his capacity of Cardinal Archbishop of Buenos Aires. See in particular *Scegliere la vita. Proposte per tempi difficili*, Milan: Bompiani, 2013.

INDEX